IDEAS
NCTM Standards-Based Instruction

Grades 5–8

IDEAS
NCTM Standards-Based Instruction

Grades 5–8

Compiled and edited

by

Michael C. Hynes

University of Central Florida
Orlando, Florida

National Council of Teachers of Mathematics
Reston, Virginia

Second printing 1997

Library of Congress Cataloging-in-Publication Data:

Ideas : NCTM standards-based instruction : grades 5–8 / compiled and
    edited by Michael C. Hynes.
        p.   cm.
    "These lessons have been selected from the 'Ideas' department in
the Arithmetic teacher: mathematics education through the middle
grades"—T.p. verso.
    Includes bibliographical references (p.   –   ).
    ISBN 0-87353-426-3 (pbk.)
    1. Mathematics—Study and teaching (Elementary)   I. Hynes,
Michael C., 1941–   . II. Arithmetic teacher.
QA135.5.I344   1996
372.7′044—dc20   96-6156
                                                                                        CIP

These lessons have been selected from the "Ideas" department in
Arithmetic Teacher: Mathematics Education through the Middle Grades.

Printed in the United States of America

Grade Levels and Publication Dates for "Ideas" Activities

Acknowledgments

The lessons selected for this publication are taken from original "Ideas" activities prepared and edited by the following:

Dianne Bankard

Anne F. Brahier

Daniel J. Brahier

Debby A. Chessin

Marea W. Channel

Rebecca B. Corwin

Yvonne M. Coston

Francis (Skip) Fennell

John Firkins

Diane M. Gard

Shirley Hodapp

Martha H. (Marty) Hopkins

Calvin Irons

Rosemary Irons

J. David Keller

Beth Kobett

Rebecca Martin

L. J. Meconi

Phyllis Knerl Miller

Barbara E. Moses

Mary Lou Nevin

Karen S. Norwood

Lisa M. Passarello

Linda Proudfit

Sherry Renga

Kay B. Sammons

Jean M. Shaw

William R. Speer

Robert Sovchik

Danna Stonecipher

Virginia Usnick

Sharon L. Young

The preparation of this manuscript was made possible through the cooperation of the Department of Instructional Programs at the University of Central Florida. Kathleen Frey provided editorial assistance and graphics preparation for drafts of the publication. Lucy Roberts was an editorial assistant throughout the project. Their efforts contributed to the quality and timely completion of this publication.

Introduction

Since its inception in 1971, the "Ideas" department has consistently been ranked as one of the most popular features of the *Arithmetic Teacher*. When the journal became known as *Arithmetic Teacher: Mathematics Education through the Middle Grades*, the popularity of "Ideas" continued. Readers of the journal find the format of student activity sheets and teacher directions to be very helpful in preparing lessons. Teachers usually copy the activity sheets for direct use in the classroom.

Early in the development of "Ideas," the lessons focused on creative paper-and-pencil activities. These activities were intended to be used to augment the textbook and make lessons more exciting. As the reform movement in mathematics education began, the feature evolved to new levels. The use of manipulatives became an important part of the lessons, and children were encouraged to use higher-order-thinking skills.

The publication of the NCTM *Curriculum and Evaluation Standards for School Mathematics* in 1989 added new aspects to the department. Without losing the friendly format, the "Ideas" lessons incorporated communication, connections, reasoning, and problem solving. Teachers saw examples of how to teach statistics and probability through "Ideas" lessons that use data sheets. In the later volumes of *Arithmetic Teacher: Mathematics Education through the Middle Grades*, teachers were given assistance in communicating with parents when Family Activities were included.

This collection of "Ideas" lessons has been compiled from the 1991–94 journals. The lessons selected were indicated by the authors to be appropriate for grades 5–8. The activity sheets may have been edited for clarity, and because of space limitations, the teacher directions may have been edited for brevity. For the reader's reference, the issue of the journal in which the original lesson appeared is noted at the bottom of the activity sheet. Family Activities and Data Sheets have been placed in separate sections. The teacher directions indicate if there is a corresponding page in these special sections.

For the reader's convenience, two reference pages are included in this publication. The first reference page is a matrix of the titles of the activities, the date of publication, and the intended grade levels for each of the activities. This page will be helpful to the teacher looking for activities for a particular grade level. Also, many teachers are seeking examples of how to incorporate ideas from the *Standards* into their lessons. The second reference page correlates the titles of the activities with the NCTM Standards that apply to the lessons. Since many of the "Ideas" lessons involve multiple Standards, teachers should review the lessons carefully to be certain that the desired emphasis on a particular Standard is present.

Standards Guide for "Ideas" Activities
Grades 5–8

	Problem Solving	Communication	Reasoning	Connections	No. and No. Relationships	No. Systems and No. Theory	Computation and Estimation	Patterns and Functions	Algebra	Statistics	Probability	Geometry	Measurement	Page Number
What Parts Do You Eat?					•								•	4
How Can You Work It?	•	•					•							6
Stamps with Patterns	•			•				•						8
The Mail Route	•		•										•	10
Tree-and-Pencil Measurements		•											•	12
Range Finder		•	•		•								•	14
What's Important about Triangles?		•	•									•	•	16
How Many Triangles Can You Construct?	•	•						•				•		18
Aluminum Cans		•		•	•					•				20
How to Bag It?		•		•						•				22
Getting the Facts		•		•									•	24
Can It Be?		•		•	•					•				26
Graphs of SKITTLES					•					•	•			28
Preference Survey									•	•	•			30
We Flip over Art			•					•				•		32
Testing the Strength of Paper Tubes		•	•							•			•	34
Spanning to the Max!	•	•		•									•	36
Super Bowl Scores				•		•	•							38
Football Finances		•	•	•			•							40
Rock 'r Rap		•								•				42
What Should We Eat?				•	•		•							44
Presidential Photo Finishes				•	•		•							46
Lewis and Clark and Me		•	•	•						•				48
Space Nutrition				•			•							50
Which Way?	•						•							52
Lock It Up	•											•		54
Computation Court: Verify the Verdict			•				•							56
Computation Court: Defend Your Decision		•	•				•							58
The World's Fastest				•			•	•						60
Weight Toss				•			•						•	62
Fraction Kites in Motion					•		•							64
High-Flying Fractions							•							66
What's the Beat?		•					•							68
Heartifacts		•					•							70
Triangles			•									•	•	72
Tessellation Combinations	•		•					•				•		76
Sports Numbers		•		•	•	•								80
Airport Numbers		•		•	•	•								82
Make a Puzzle		•										•	•	84
Triangular Regions Make Many Figures		•										•		86
Name Your Tune		•								•				88
History of Populations		•		•	•					•				90
Heights of Students in Our Class										•			•	92
About Our Class										•				94
Television Commercials		•								•				96
Television Viewing Time		•					•							98
Fingerprint Detective	•			•			•							100

IDEAS

Activity Sheets

IDEAS

What Parts Do You Eat?

LEVELS 5–6

Background

Manufactured packaging and nature's packaging serve many functions. They help to keep foods from decomposing and protect foods from breakage as well as bacteria. Manufactured packaging often advertises products and distinguishes them from others of the same type. Printed nutritional information informs consumers and helps them buy appropriate amounts. Packaging also adds to the weight and cost of foods. After using the product, people have to dispose of the packaging.

Objectives

Students will weigh packaged foods and packaging materials; they will determine what fraction of the total weight is attributable to packaging.

Directions

1. Ask half the class to bring in a nutritious snack wrapped in its manufactured packaging. Ask the other half to bring in whole fruits. A fruit with an easily removed peel is preferable.

2. Discuss with the class the reasons for packaging. Encourage them to speculate about the weight of their packaged food and whether the packaging is a large or small fraction of its total weight.

3. Organize the students into groups of five. Two in each group should have snacks with manufactured packaging; two others should have fruit; the fifth student may have either one.

4. Give each group the "What Parts Do You Eat?" activity sheet. Be sure that students know what data they are to

Prepared by Debby A. Chessin *and* Jean M. Shaw
Edited by John Firkins

record. Discuss with the students the data they might record in the blank last column. Perhaps they could state whether each fraction or decimal is closer to 0, 1/2, or 1. They might be able to determine, using a calculator or pencil and paper, the percent for each fraction or decimal. They might write the ratio of the weight of the edible part of their snacks to the total weight.

5. Set up a system so that groups can take turns using a balance scale and gram weights to find the total weight of the item and the weight of the packaging. Help the students decide what to do with weights that are too small to register on the scale—small cellophane wrappers, for example. They might record "zero" or "negligible" or "too light to measure." Encourage group members to take turns using the scales and to check one another's answers.

6. As they determine the weight of the edible parts of their snacks, the students will need to remove the snacks from their containers and place them on plastic wrap or clean paper towels. Appoint a person in each group to be in charge of these supplies.

7. Allow time for the students to discuss the questions at the bottom of the activity sheet. Perhaps one student can take notes for each group. Invite group members to share their ideas with the class.

Extensions

1. Lead the children in examining and discussing the nutritional information found on most manufactured packaging. On the basis of this information, determine which snacks brought by the students are the most nutritious. Help the students interpret the nutrition information, such as percents of

recommended daily allowances. Some may be interested in the percents of such items as fat content.

2. Let interested students research and present the nutritional value of the various fruit snacks brought in by their classmates.

3. Have the students find the prices of their snacks and determine which snacks have the least amount of packaging for the price.

4. Invite the students to display packaging material. Ask them to label their items according to the purpose—health and safety, attractiveness and advertising, consumer information, and so on.

5. Let the students compare nature's packaging, such as fruit peels, with manufactured packaging. What do they have in common?

6. How can students determine the weight of packaging materials that are too light to register on the scale? Let the students discuss possible methods. Perhaps they can get several wrappers of the same kind, use the scale to determine their total weight, then divide by the number of wrappers to get the approximate weight of a single wrapper. What other methods can the students propose?

7. Follow up after a week on any students' plans for changing their purchasing habits on the basis of what they found in the activity. Have they discussed their findings with adults? Have they acted on their plans? How?

What Parts Do You Eat?

Names _____

_____

_____

_____

Many foods are packaged in plastic, aluminum, and other materials. Packaging material adds to the weight and cost of many manufactured foods. Nature's packaging, such as fruit peels, also adds to the weight.

Investigate the weights of manufactured packaging and nature's packaging. Complete the chart with your group.

Product	Total Weight	Weight of Packaging	Weight of Packaging / Total Weight	

Talk about your findings. What do you notice about the fractions in the chart? _____

_____

What did you know before you started to investigate? _____

_____

What did you learn? Did anything surprise you? What? _____

_____

What additional investigations did you plan? _____

_____

What did your group do best as you worked? What might you improve if you worked together again? _____

_____

Did you find anything that might make you reconsider or change your buying habits? What?_____

_____

From the *Arithmetic Teacher*, May 1994

IDEAS

How Can You Work It?

LEVELS 7–8

Background

Many students and adults drink daily from aluminum cans. These cans are sturdy, lightweight, and inexpensive. The introduction of attached pop tops and the ease of recycling have made aluminum cans attractive to many advocates of a cleaner, safer environment.

This activity involves problem solving based on measurement data and is intended to draw students' attention to the large number of cans that people use.

Objectives

Students will work together to solve a problem on the basis of measurement data, analyze their work, and use factual material to write problems for others to solve.

Directions

1. Organize students into groups of three to five. Distribute the "How Can You Work It?" activity sheet to each group.

2. Have students read and discuss the problem and fill in the first four boxes as they work. Students will need to determine the height of a single softdrink can (about 12 cm, or 4 3/4 in.) and the height of the classroom. They will also need to find the distance from the earth to the moon. You may wish to have students research this fact in a reference or science book, or you may want to give the students these data: The distance from the earth to the moon at perigee, its closest point, is approximately 350 000 km (220 000

mi.); at apogee, the point at which the earth and moon are farthest apart, the distance is about 400 000 km (250 000 mi.) (Victor and Kellough 1993). Students are likely to find that approximately 8 300 cans are required for a height of 1 000 meters and that more than 3 billion cans are needed to reach the moon.

3. Have students discuss their final answers and the processes they used to arrive at those answers.

4. Answers from groups of students are likely to vary. Let them speculate on the reasons for these variations. Perhaps the measurements on which they based their calculations were different; perhaps some rounded numbers, whereas others did not. Encourage group members to share whether, and how, they used the calculator to work on the problem.

5. Invite the students to use the "facts about aluminum cans" information to create one or more problems for another group to solve. Students should show the answers to their problems on the back of the activity sheet.

6. Allow time for groups to exchange problems with other groups, solve the problems, discuss answers, and explain their thinking.

Extensions

1. Help the students develop a class project of collecting and recycling cans and deciding how to spend any money they make. Encourage predicting and record keeping as students carry out the project.

2. Have the students gather data on the number of cans that they and their family members use in a day, a week, and a

month. Let them organize, display, and compare their data. Would the total height of the cans used by the class in a month reach to the ceiling? To a height of 1 000 meters? To the moon?

3. Have the students research alternatives to cans for packaging drinks. They might read about different kinds of packaging and their pros and cons. The students might look for alternatives at grocery stores as well as talk to store personnel about packaging alternatives. On the basis of their findings, students could organize a debate about what kind of packaging they believe is best.

4. Students might find data on other environmental concerns and create problems based on these data for their classmates.

References

Javna, John. *Fifty Simple Things Kids Can Do to Save the Earth.* Kansas City, Mo.: Earthworks Group, 1990.

Lord, Suzanne. *Garbage: The Trashiest Book You'll Ever Read.* New York: Scholastic Books, 1993.

Victor, Edward, and Richard Kellough. *Science in the Elementary School.* New York: Macmillan, 1993.

World Book Encyclopedia. Chicago: World Book, 1991.

Prepared by Debby A. Chessin *and* Jean M. Shaw
Edited by John Firkins

How Can You Work It?

Problem: Most people use many 355-ml (12 oz.) cans each day. Imagine cans piled on top of one another. How many cans would it take to reach the ceiling? To reach 1000 m high? To reach the moon?

Read the questions. Record your ideas as you discuss the problem.

Understanding the problem
With what is the problem concerned? What data are given? What must we find? What sort of answers are we seeking? Will a picture, chart, or model help?

Making a plan
How might we get the work done? Should we try out our plan on a simpler problem? Should we use another strategy?

Doing the work
How can we cooperate to get the work done? Will we use a calculator? How?

Looking back
Do our results seem reasonable? How do our results compare with what we expected? Why do we think we're right? Do we need to redo all or just parts? How well did we work together?

On the basis of these facts and others, write a problem for another group.

Facts about aluminum cans

- It takes 4–6 tons of bauxite (aluminum ore) to make 1 ton of aluminum (*World Book Encyclopedia* 1991).

- A typical aluminum can weighs about 18 g.

- A typical American family uses 1500 aluminum cans a year (Javna 1990).

- In your community when people recycle cans, they get $ ____ per pound.

- A typical American family throws away about 540 pounds of metal each year (Lord 1993).

Write your answer and explain the way you solved it on the back of this activity sheet.

From the *Arithmetic Teacher*, May 1994

IDEAS

Stamps with Patterns

LEVELS 4–6

Literature

Jacobsen, Karen. *Stamps*. Chicago: Children's Press, 1983.

United States Postal Service. *The Postal Service Guide to U.S. Stamps*. Washington, D.C.: USPS, 1992.

Background

The stamps in groups 1, 2, and 5, which are reproduced on the activity sheet, are from *The Postal Service Guide to U.S. Stamps* (United States Postal Service 1992, pp. 275, 187, and 191, respectively). The other stamps shown are reproduced from actual stamps. The stamps in group 1 are classified as Indian Headdresses; those in groups 2 and 5 are classified as American Folk Art: Pueblo Pottery and American Folk Art: Quilts, respectively.

The classification given to stamps by the United States Postal Service can be found in The Postal Service Guide to U.S. Stamps; this book is available at local post offices in the United States. The local library probably has books on stamps written both for children and for adults; see Stamps by Karen Jacobsen (1983).

Objectives

Students observe a variety of stamps with patterns and assign categories for classifying the stamps. They conduct research to determine classifications used by the postal service in various countries to classify stamps. They design an original stamp with a pattern.

Directions

1. Distribute a copy of the activity sheet "Stamps with Patterns" to each student. Divide the students into groups of four. Guide the students in describing the pattern found on each stamp.

2. Ask the students to follow the instructions to complete the activity sheet.

3. After the students have designed their own stamps, make copies of each student's stamp. Have each group of students sort and classify the stamps from the entire class. In a whole-group setting, discuss the classifications submitted by each group and guide the students in forming a consensus about the final categories to be used for classifying the stamps; as a whole-class activity, sort the stamps using these categories. Make a bulletin board with the students' stamps, using their classification scheme.

4. Encourage the students to search for other stamps that have patterns.

Applicable Standards

- **Problem Solving**
- **Connections**
- **Patterns and Functions**

Prepared by Sherry Renga
Edited by John Firkins

Stamps with Patterns

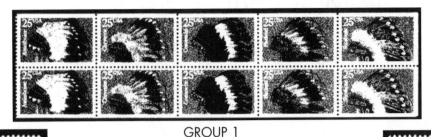

GROUP 1

GROUP 2

GROUP 3

GROUP 4

GROUP 5

A. Give a name to each group of stamps to describe how you would classify them. The first one is completed for you.

1. Group 1 __Indian Headdresses_____

2. Group 2 _____

3. Group 3 _____

4. Group 4 _____

5. Group 5 _____

B. Conduct research to determine some of the different types of stamps that are available in your country. Name at least three different classifications of stamps. _____

_____

_____

C. Make your own stamp using some type of pattern. Determine how you would classify your stamp.

The Mail Route

Literature

Roth, Harold. *First Class! The Postal System in Action.* New York: Pantheon Books, 1983.

Background

First Class! The Postal System in Action (Roth 1983) is written for students in grades 3 through 7. It describes how the United States postal system works.

Objectives

Given a map representing a postal route, the students read the map and solve the problem of determining the shortest path that they could follow to deliver mail on this route. They draw to scale an enlargement of the given map.

Directions

1. Read aloud *First Class! The Postal System in Action.*

2. Distribute a copy of the activity sheet "The Mail Route" to each student. Divide the class into groups of four. Ask the students to imagine that they are mail carriers and their job is to carry mail to families on all the streets shown. Tell the students that on the map shown, the length of Buena Vista Street from Chestnut Street to W. 6th Street is approximately 2150 feet; thus, each block is approximately 358 feet

long. (You may wish to take your class outside and measure 358 feet.) Two houses are located on each side on each block on Buena Vista Street. Houses on the other streets on the map can be assumed to be approximately the same distance apart as those on Buena Vista Street.

3. Discuss the questions on the activity sheet.

   a) For items 1 and 2, encourage the students to make assumptions about the number of houses on each block, the length of each block, and whether they would go back and forth across the street or go down one side of the street then go up the other side.

   b) For item 3, the students need to plan where they would start and end the route, where they would park the mail truck, and how much mail they would carry before returning to the truck.

4. Have each group of students complete the activity sheet and form a consensus about the shortest route. Give each group a large sheet of butcher paper and have them reproduce the map on a larger scale; it should be large enough so they can use it to demonstrate their "shortest route" to the entire class.

5. Ask each group to share their "shortest route" with the class and to justify it. Conduct a whole-class discussion on the findings of the various groups.

Extension

Enlarge the map on the activity sheet to make a bulletin board. As a whole-class activity, have the students place houses (stickers of houses would be great!) where they might be in a real town, place a name on each house to represent one person who lives there, and assign an address to each house. Have each group of students address an envelope (a 3×5 card works well) to a person at each house and arrange the envelopes in the order in which they would be delivered. Compare the results among different groups.

Applicable Standards

- **Problem Solving**
- **Reasoning**
- **Measurement**

Prepared by Sherry Renga
Edited by John Firkins

The Mail Route

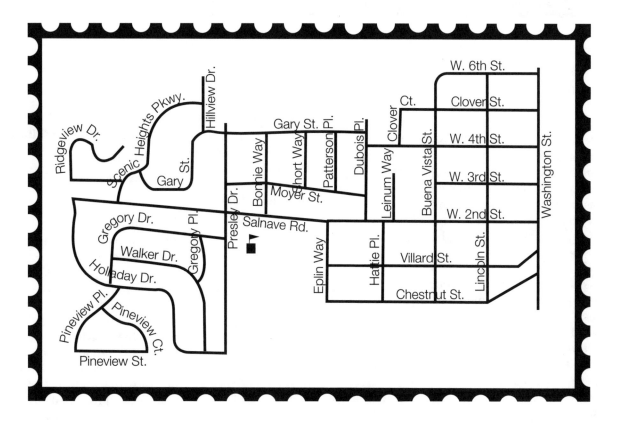

Assume that you are a mail carrier and have a walking route. You must deliver mail to both sides of each street shown.

1. What information do you need before you can plan your route? _____
_____
_____

2. What assumptions do you need to make? _____
_____

3. Describe a route that you might take to deliver mail to the houses on each street listed. Include your starting and ending points and the order in which you would walk the route. (Use crayons or colored pencils to help you keep track of your route.) _____
_____
_____
_____

4. Describe the shortest route that you could take. _____
_____
_____
_____

From the *Arithmetic Teacher*, April 1994

Tree-and-Pencil Measurements

LEVELS 5–6

Background

This indirect-measuring technique easily connects measurement to the real world of the outdoors, where practical considerations sometimes prevent direct measurement. Suppose we want to measure the height of a tree. (This approach is appropriate for flag, light, and telephone poles, also.)

Sight the top of a tree by holding a pencil vertically about 30 cm from your face. Close one eye and line up the tip of the pencil and the top of the tree. Move forward or backward until the tip of the pencil is at the top of the tree and the eraser-end of the pencil is at the base of the tree (see fig. 1).

Next, rotate the pencil so that it is parallel to the ground and at a right angle to the line of sight from your eye to the tree. Be sure that the eraser end is still visually aligned with the base of the tree. Have a partner stand away from the tree, again at a right angle to the line of sight. Have the partner line up his or her feet with the tip of the pencil (see fig. 2). Measure the distance from the tree to your partner with a meterstick or trundle wheel. This distance is the approximate height of the tree.

Objectives

To use an indirect-measurement system to determine the height of such inaccessible objects as trees, flagpoles, or buildings; to practice measurement with a meterstick or trundle wheel

Materials

- A "Tree-and-Pencil Measurements" activity sheet for each student
- Metersticks or trundle wheels
- Pencils

Applicable Standards

- **Communication**
- **Measurement**

Directions

Distribute an activity sheet to each student. Demonstrate the use of the pencil-sighting method by finding the height of the ceiling of the classroom. It is best to find the height at a corner of the room. Have students pair up and repeat the activity. Discuss any problems as a group. Then proceed outdoors. Have several pairs of students measure the same object (tree, flagpole, peak of roof, and so on) and compare their results. Have each student complete the activity sheet, then have each pair write a summary of the experiment.

Prepared by Robert Sovchik *and* L. J. Meconi
Edited by John Firkins

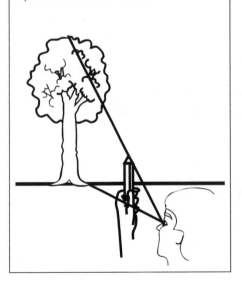

FIGURE 1

Align the pencil's tip and eraser with the top and bottom of the tree.

FIGURE 2

Rotate the pencil so that it is parallel to the ground and at a right angle to the line of sight. Align partner with the tip of the pencil.

Tree-and-Pencil Measurements

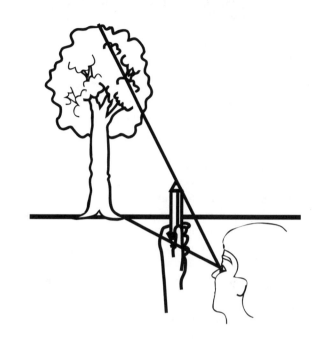

Work with a partner. Measure the height of a corner of your classroom using the directions given by your teacher. Record your results below, then swap roles with your partner and measure again. How close are you? Are your results reasonable? Are they similar to your classmates' results?

Go outside and use the same method to measure the height of something you can't measure directly—a tree, a flagpole, the rooftop, or the like. Reverse roles with your partner and measure again. Do your estimates match? Are they close? Record your results below.

1. The classroom is about _____ meters high.

2. The object we measured is a _____. Its approximate height is _____ m.

Think about the following questions and write the answers.

3. What are some other things whose heights you could estimate this way? _____

_____

_____

_____

4. What are some factors that keep this method from being an accurate way to measure? _____

_____

_____

_____

_____

_____

_____

From the *Arithmetic Teacher*, January 1994

IDEAS

Range Finder

Background

Developing proportional reasoning is an important conceptual goal. Students reason proportionally when solving percent problems and in beginning algebra. Indirect measurement also presents a way to experience proportionality. This activity offers an alternative method of indirect distance measurement. Practice in reading a ruler and computing with rational numbers are ancillary benefits of this activity.

Objectives

Students will use proportionality when sighting objects at different distances and compute a solution to a proportional-measurement situation in which equal ratios are used.

Materials

• A paper clip and ruler for each group

Prepared by Robert Sovchik *and* L. J. Meconi
Edited by John Firkins

• A "Range Finder" activity sheet for each student

Directions

1. Give each small group a paper clip and a ruler.

2. Follow the construction directions and proportional-reasoning instructions on the "Range Finder" activity sheet.

3. Review methods for solving a proportion. For example, if $n/2 = 4/8$, $8n = 8$, and $n = 1$.

4. Take the class outside. Try several examples of indirect measurement with the class. For example, suppose a student is sighted completely at the 4-cm mark. Use a meterstick or trundle wheel to measure the actual distance from the observer to the person (see fig. 1). Next have the person move back to an unknown distance (see fig. 2). Again have the person with the range finder sight the other individual. Suppose that now the person is completely

Applicable Standards
• **Communication**
• **Reasoning**
• **Number and Number Relationships**
• **Measurement**

framed at the 10-cm mark; $4/6 = 10/x$ is a correct proportion with x being the distance from the person to the observer. Simplifying, $4x = 60$; $x = 15$. So the person is situated 15 meters from the observer with the range finder.

5. Discuss this practical example of proportionality with the class.

Extension

Repeat this activity two or three times. A useful communication extension is to have students invent a situation in which this activity is used and then write a brief paragraph describing the measurement techniques used.

FIGURE 1

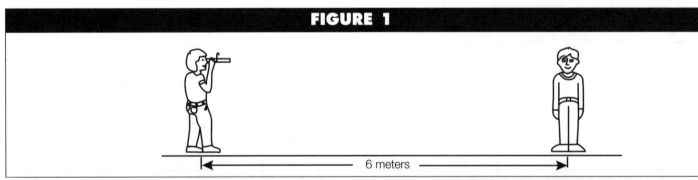

6 meters

FIGURE 2

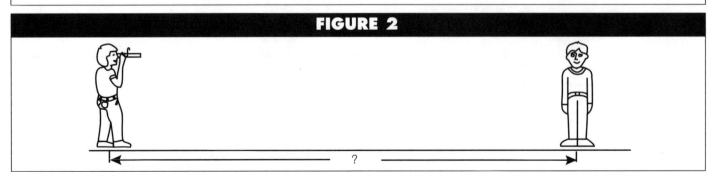

?

Range Finder

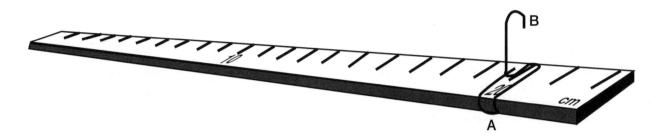

Use a ruler and a paper clip to make a range finder. Bend one end of the paper clip so that it wraps around the ruler and slides easily along its length. (See A in the diagram.) Bend the other end of the paper clip into a small semicircle. (See B.) Slide the paper clip to the 20-cm mark on the ruler. Have someone stand at the other end of the room. Adjust the semicircle so that it exactly frames the other person's face when you sight along the ruler from the "zero" end.

1. Determine the distance from you to your partner. Have the person come halfway back to you. Slide the paper clip to the 10-cm mark. Does the semicircle frame the face? Should it?

2. Go outside. Have a classmate stand a *known* distance from you. Sight the student completely in your range finder. Record the paper clip's position as your first sighting distance and construct the ratio of

    first sighting distance:known distance.

    Have your classmate move farther away. Again, sight the student completely in your range finder. Your paper clip's position is your second sighting distance. Equate the two ratios and find the unknown distance.

$$\frac{\text{First sighting distance}}{\text{Known distance}} = \frac{\text{Second sighting distance}}{\text{Unknown distance}}$$

3. Try other examples with your range finder. How accurate is it? Write a paragraph describing how you determined the accuracy of your range finder. _____

    _____

    _____

    _____

First sighting distance	Known distance	Second sighting distance	Unknown distance

From the *Arithmetic Teacher*, January 1994

IDEAS

What's Important about Triangles?

LEVELS 4–5

Objective

Students discover when it is, or is not, possible to make triangles from given lengths of construction paper. They conclude that the sum of the lengths of any two sides must be greater than the length of the third side.

Materials

- Activity sheet "What's Important about Triangles?"
- Tape, scissors
- Spinner with numbers 1–6 for the extension activity

Directions

1. Duplicate the activity sheet on construction paper.

2. Students measure, fold, and tape each strip to make a triangle, if possible.

3. During a class discussion, ask students to tell what happened when they made the triangles:

- Which measurements were possible?
- What discoveries were made about the lengths of the sides of the triangles?
- Could you categorize the triangles as equilateral, isosceles, or scalene?

Answers

A. yes, B. yes, C. no, D. yes, E. no, F. no, G. yes, H. yes

Extension

Students can sort the triangles as they work in small groups. Have each person make four triangles, *A*, *B*, *C*, and *D*. To determine the lengths of the sides of the triangles, each person spins three times for each triangle and then makes the sides match the measurements that were spun. The group decides how to sort all the triangles. Then they design a graph to organize and record the data. They write a newspaper article that explains the results. The articles could be compiled to form a class *Math Newspaper*. Information could include the number of congruent triangles in each category, the number of different triangles in each category, the longest and shortest perimeters, and other discoveries.

Students can investigate the following challenges:

- How many isosceles triangles can be made with a perimeter of 24 cm if each side must be a whole number of centimeters? (Ans.: 5 triangles. The

sides of the triangles would be 11, 11, and 2; 10, 10, and 4; 9, 9, and 6; 8, 8, and 8; and 7, 7, and 10.)

- What patterns did you notice for the length of the unequal side?
- What happens if your triangle has a different perimeter, such as 20 cm, 21 cm, 22 cm, 23 cm,…, 30 cm?

Family Activity

See "Let's Work Together" on page 110.

Prepared by Marea W. Channel
Edited by John Firkins

What's Important about Triangles?

Make important discoveries about triangles by measuring and taping strips of construction paper together. Choose a partner. Use the measurements below to make the triangles *A* to *H*. Cut out 1-cm-by-18-cm strips from the centimeter graph paper. Measure, fold, and tape a strip together to construct a triangle. Be sure to label each triangle.

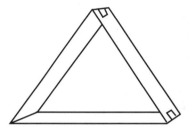

A: 6 cm, 6 cm, 6 cm   C: 4 cm, 9 cm, 5 cm   E: 4 cm, 4 cm, 8 cm   G: 5 cm, 5 cm, 8 cm
B: 6 cm, 7 cm, 4 cm   D: 7 cm, 4 cm, 7 cm   F: 7 cm, 4 cm, 2 cm   H: 4 cm, 4 cm, 4 cm

Compare and talk about the discoveries you made. By the way, you have been invited to appear on a television talk show to explain what you learned from this experiment. Write a script for your presentation.

Centimeter Graph Paper

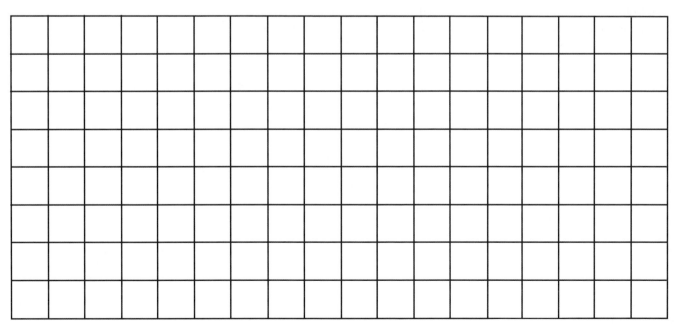

From the *Arithmetic Teacher*, November 1993

How Many Triangles Can You Construct?

LEVELS 6–8

Objective

Students become actively engaged in mathematical experiments to discover and describe number patterns that unfold when they construct triangles within a large triangle.

Materials

- Copy of the activity sheet "How Many Triangles Can You Construct?"
- Ruler, pencils, or fine-line markers
- Writing paper

Directions

1. Duplicate and follow the directions on the activity sheet.

2. Ask questions to stimulate class discussion.

- How did your triangle change?
- How did you find out the number of triangles that were possible?
- What did you notice about the number patterns?

3. Suppose you are a news reporter for a major television station. What questions would you ask a mathematician about the number patterns in the triangles?

4. Suppose that your readers want you to describe the changes that occurred in the second triangle. What would you write in your newspaper column?

Answers

Triangle A

Stage	Number of triangles
1	1
2	4
3	16
4	64

Triangle B

Stage	Number of shaded triangles		
1	3	$(4-1)$	$3 \times 1 = 3$
2	9	$(12-3)$	$3 \times 3 = 9$
3	27	$(36-9)$	$3 \times 9 = 27$
4	81	$(108-27)$	$3 \times 27 = 81$

Extensions

1. Give each student another copy of the worksheet. Ask students to predict

and then determine what happens if they—

- divide each side of the triangle into thirds and then connect the points of trisection;
- repeat the process again.

2. Ask the students, as young mathematicians, to write about the procedures and results of the experiment.

Family Activity

See "Let's Work Together" on page 110.

Prepared by Marea W. Channel
Edited by John Firkins

How Many Triangles Can You Construct?

The midpoints of each side of triangle *A* have been joined. Find out what happens if you repeat the process successively several times. How many triangles do you think you would get? With a partner, try this experiment. Create a table and write a paragraph that describes what you discover in the number patterns.

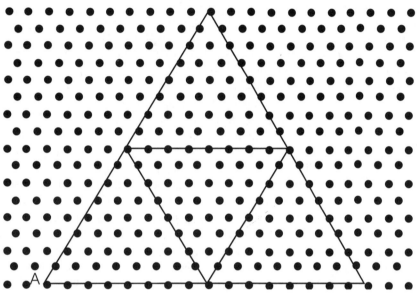

The midpoints of triangle *B* have been joined during the first stage of this mathematical experiment. Shade in the middle triangle, then join the midpoints of the sides of the unshaded triangles. Repeat the process for at least two more stages. What patterns do you think will emerge? Compare the size of the triangles. How far do you think you can take this process? What conclusions can you draw from these experiments?

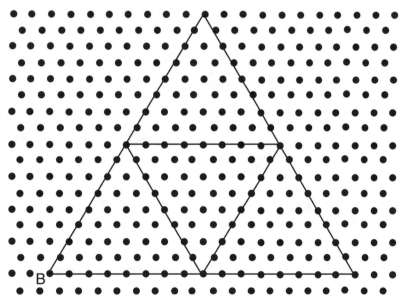

From the *Arithmetic Teacher*, November 1993

IDEAS

Aluminum Cans

LEVELS 5–6

Background

People drink soda, juices, tea, and other beverages from aluminum cans. These cans are fairly inexpensive to produce, but since aluminum can be recycled, much material and energy could be saved if people would recycle their cans and other aluminum products regularly.

Objectives

To gather and graph data; to interpret data, including figuring and displaying the mean of a set of data; to develop a plan for future actions

Directions

1. Show an aluminum can. Discuss what students know about such cans. Of what are they made? What products are sold in similar cans? What other products are made of aluminum? Why is aluminum a valuable metal? (It's relatively inexpensive, malleable, and lightweight.)

2. Explain the directions for making the graph on the "Aluminum Cans" activity sheet. Allow time for students to record their own numbers, poll four classmates, and graph the data.

3. Have each student look at the graph and write several things the graph shows. Students should note the range of numbers on their graphs. Review, as needed, how to figure a mean average. Have students use a calculator, mental mathematics, or pencil and paper to figure the mean average of their sets of data, then graph the results.

4. Discuss ways to compare an individual's can use in a day with the typical American's use of 1500 cans each year (Javna 1990). Have students compute

Prepared by Jean M. Shaw
Edited by John Firkins

their yearly use and compare it with 1500. They should also work with the group mean, figure the number of cans used each year on the basis of this number, and compare the yearly number with 1500. Students should use calculators and may check each other's work.

5. Students should discuss some things they learned from the activity. Were they surprised at their own use or the mean for the people they polled? What did they learn about the mean compared with individual numbers in their data sets?

6. Have students work individually or in small groups to discuss and write plans for conserving aluminum. A committee should post examples of the plans; alternatively, have students report the plans to the class.

Answers

Students' graphs will vary according to the data collected.

1. Each student should write at least three things about the graph. The greatest and least number stated should match those shown on the graph. Students can check each other's computations of the mean. Unless all the numbers on a graph are the same, the mean will be somewhere between the lowest and highest number, though not necessarily in the middle.

2–3. Answers will vary. Most students will multiply their daily number of cans by 365 or 365.25 to figure their approximate yearly can use. They should multiply the group mean by 365 or 365.25 to figure the mean number of cans used yearly, keeping in mind that can use is probably greater in the warm-weather months than in winter months. The time of the year the survey is done may skew the results. Comparisons of the

Applicable Standards

* **Communication**
* **Connections**
* **Number and Number Relationships**
* **Statistics**

students' numbers with 1500 will vary.

4. Students' recycling plans will vary.

Extensions

1. Have students gather data for the number of aluminum cans they use each day for a week. They can find the mean number for these data and compare it with the "yesterday's number" used for the graph and with the group mean found on the graph.

Have students discuss whether "yesterday's number" or their weekly mean was more typical of the number of cans they use.

2. Let students compile similar data for their family's use of aluminum cans.

3. Start or expand a school project for recycling cans.

4. Have students write and solve problems on the basis of current aluminum-recycling prices in the community.

5. Estimate the number of aluminum cans that might be collected in a given area. Organize a can cleanup and discuss and enforce safety rules. Compare the number of cans collected with the estimates.

Family Activity

See "Plastic Packaging" on page 112.

Reference

Javna, John. *Fifty Simple Things Kids Can Do to Save the Earth*. Kansas City, Mo.: Andrews & McMeel, 1990.

Aluminum Cans

It is common to see people drinking or pouring drinks from aluminum cans. How many cans do you and your classmates ordinarily use in a day? Let's find out. Think back about the number of cans you used yesterday. Show that number on the graph. Ask four classmates about the number of aluminum cans they used yesterday, too. Record these data on the graph.

Name	How Many Aluminum Cans Did You Use Yesterday?
Mean of Data	

0 1 2 3 4 5 6 7 8 9 10 11 12
Number of Cans Used

1. Write about the graph you made. What are some things it shows? What was the greatest number of cans that was used? The least? What was the mean number of cans used? Figure this number and fill it in on the graph. Discuss some things you notice about the mean and the other numbers on the graph. _____

_____

_____

_____

2. *Fifty Simple Things Kids Can Do to Save the Earth* (Javna 1990) states that a typical American uses 1500 aluminum cans each year. On the basis of the number of cans you used yesterday, figure the number of cans you might use in a year. How does your number compare with 1500? _____

3. Use the daily mean from your graph to determine a yearly mean. Compare this number with 1500. _____

_____

4. Aluminum cans can be recycled many times, which allows more of the metal to be used for airplanes, bicycles, and building materials. Less energy is used. Write some things you might do to recycle or conserve aluminum. _____

_____

_____

_____

From the *Arithmetic Teacher*, September 1993

How to Bag It?

LEVELS 7–8

Objectives

To record notes from a discussion on pros and cons of kinds of bags, to gather data and make and interpret a graph, to develop a recycling plan

Directions

1. Distribute a copy of the "How to Bag It?" activity sheet to each student. Have students read the information at the top and encourage them to add to it on the basis of their own experience and reading.

2. Organize the class into groups of three to five students. Ask them to discuss the pros and cons of using different kinds of bags and record some of their notes in the chart. Ask them to discuss using other kinds of bags or ways of wrapping purchases for the "other" category. They might also include in this category the strategy of refusing bags for small purchases.

3. Ask each group to note some especially good ideas. Have group representatives share this material with the class.

4. Review different kinds of graphs with the class. Mention previously studied graph types—bar graphs, picture graphs, circle graphs, box-and-whiskers graphs, scatterplots, and others—and their purposes. Ask students to poll ten classmates concerning the type of bag each considers best on the basis of the previous discussion. Each student should decide on a graph that will best show the data.

5. Allow students the time to poll ten classmates and graph the type of bag each has chosen.

6. Have students answer question 3

concerning their choices of types of graphs. They should meet in groups and critique each other's choice of type.

7. Have each student complete question 4 and check it with a partner. As the students work, circulate and listen to the discussions. Spot-check some of the students' work to ensure that it is reasonable and accurate. Have students show their graphs to the class and share some of their interpretive statements.

8. Lead students in brainstorming ways to use their bags with conservation in mind and ways that disposable bags can be reused and recycled. On the basis of the discussion, ask each student to make a plan for limiting the use of bags.

9. Appoint a committee of students to display the worksheets in the classroom or in the hall for others to see. You might also want to display these worksheets at a local grocery store.

Answers

Answers will vary depending on students' opinions. They may show their data in picture or bar graphs using three or four categories, as suggested in the pros-and-cons chart. They might have chosen a circle graph to show each respondent's opinion as part of the ten responses that were gathered.

Extensions

1. Ask students to include in their graph interpretation statements about fractions, decimals, and percents.

2. Talk with students about what aspects would constitute a good job of completing the worksheet. Establish some criteria, perhaps including such items as these: each group member contributed ideas, the group carefully selected a best idea to share with the

Applicable Standards

- **Communication**
- **Connections**
- **Statistics**

class, choices of graph types were carefully made, graphs were neatly and accurately made on the basis of data, several interpretive statements were made. Have students use the criteria to self- or peer-evaluate their work.

3. A fifteen-year-old tree is required to make approximately 700 grocery bags. How long will these bags last in a grocery store? Have students decide on ways to research the answer, then carry out their plans for a homework assignment.

4. Ask students to share with several people outside the classroom the results of their discussion on the pros and cons of using different kinds of bags. They could discuss their opinions with family members or friends in other classes. After presenting the information, the students should ask several people about the best kind of bag and graph their results. Students can compare the data gathered from those queried with that from classmates and post their graphs in the classroom.

5. Plastic-bag manufacturers claim that a plastic grocery bag uses about one-sixth as much raw material as does a paper grocery bag. Have students bring in several bags of each kind, then weigh them and calculate the average weight for each. Do their findings approximate the 1:6 ratio?

Family Activity

See "Plastic Packaging" on page 112.

Prepared by Jean M. Shaw
Edited by John Firkins

Name _____

How to Bag It?

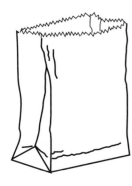

Most purchases are bagged in plastic or paper. Environmentally aware people question whether so many bags are needed. They remind us of such facts as the following: A fifteen-year-old tree makes only 700 grocery bags. Plastic bags, typically discarded, take up little landfill space but don't biodegrade. Some people, like those in other countries, take their own plastic or cloth bags to carry their purchases. Others "just say no" to bags for small purchases, telling the store clerk they don't need a bag.

1. What are some pros and cons of using different kinds of bags? Discuss this question with a group. Make notes in the chart.

Type of bag	Pros	Cons
Paper bags		
Plastic bags		
Reusable bags		
Other		

2. After your discussion, poll ten classmates to see which kind of bag they think is best to use. Choose a type of graph. Show your data in a graph sketched in the space to the right.

3. What made you choose the type of graph you made? _____
_____

4. Interpret your graph. Write several things the graph shows. _____
_____
_____

5. On the basis of your discussion and of what you found in your poll of classmates, think of a plan to conserve energy and material associated with manufacturing bags. Summarize your plan below. _____
_____
_____
_____
_____

From the *Arithmetic Teacher*, September 1993

IDEAS

Getting the Facts

LEVELS 4–5

Literature

Clement, Rod. *Counting on Frank*. Milwaukee, Wis.: Gareth Stevens Children's Books, 1991. ISBN 0-8368-0358-2.

Story summary

The narrator likes to collect facts with the help of his dog, Frank. Each two-page spread of this book includes a different fact involving such mathematical topics as counting, size comparison, and ratio, along with delightful illustrations.

Objective

Students solve problems involving estimation of volume. (Because this activity requires data collection and a great deal of problem solving, it may not be completed in one class period.)

Materials

• *Counting on Frank* by Rod Clement
• Copy of activity sheet "Getting the Facts"
• Calculators (optional)

Directions

1. Read the entire story aloud.

2. Tell students that they will be doing an activity sheet that requires them to know the size of the average humpback whale. Discuss where this information can be found.

3. After the information is found, divide the class into small, cooperative working groups. Provide each group with a copy of the activity sheet "Getting the Facts."

4. Ask students to calculate how large a box is needed to hold the average humpback whale. Because the data they have collected will most likely include weight and length, students will have to make inferences about several dimensions of the box. These decisions should be justified on the activity sheet.

5. After estimating the size of the boy's house, encourage each group to describe the process they used to find the answer.

Applicable Standards

• **Communication**
• **Connections**
• **Measurement**

6. Discuss the information needed to determine the number of whales that would fit inside the school.

7. Direct each group to complete the activity sheet.

Prepared by Martha H. (Marty) Hopkins
Edited by William R. Speer *and* Daniel J. Brahier

Name _____

Getting the Facts

One of the facts shared in the book *Counting on Frank* is that only ten humpback whales would fit in the narrator's house. Let's find out the size of his house.

Getting the Facts
How big is the average humpback whale? _____

Using the Facts
If you placed one whale inside a box, about how big would the box need to be?

Length ————————————

Width————————————

Height ————————————

Describe how you determined the dimensions of the box. _____

_____

_____

About how much space would ten boxes fill?_____

About how big is the boy's house?_____

About how many humpback whales would fit in your school? _____

Write down how you arrived at your answer. _____

_____

_____

_____

_____

From the *Arithmetic Teacher*, May 1993

Can It Be?

Literature

Juster, Norton. *The Phantom Tollbooth*. New York: Random House, 1961. ISBN 0-394-82199-8.

Story summary

Milo and his watchdog, Tock, travel through Dictionopolis and Digitopolis in this delightful fantasy. Milo's mission is to reunite the princesses of Dictionopolis (Rhyme) and Digitopolis (Reason) so that the world will once again have rhyme and reason. While completing his mission, Milo and his companions experience many language and mathematical concepts.

Objective

Students explore and interpret the concept of averages.

Materials

- *The Phantom Tollbooth* by Norton Juster
- Copy of activity sheet "Can It Be?"
- Newspapers

Directions

1. Read the entire book aloud.

2. Discuss the meaning of averaging as a leveling process. Ask students to identify situations when they have experienced averaging in the past (grades, baseball statistics, and so on).

3. Distribute copies of the activity sheet "Can It Be?"

4. Direct students to read each scenario from *The Phantom Tollbooth* and to write their explanations in the spaces provided. Encourage students to share their responses in a class discussion.

5. Discuss places where averages might be found in the newspaper.

6. Distribute newspapers.

7. Direct students to complete the activity sheet and discuss responses.

Applicable Standards

- **Communication**
- **Connections**
- **Number and Number Relationships**
- **Statistics**

Extension

Ask students to find other discussions of averaging in *The Phantom Tollbooth* and to decide if Milo's friends are telling him the truth.

Prepared by Martha H. (Marty) Hopkins
Edited by William R. Speer *and* Daniel J. Brahier

Can It Be?

In *The Phantom Tollbooth*, 0.58 of a child tells Milo that being a fraction of a person is really quite lucky. He says, "Every average family has 2.58 children, so I always have someone to play with." Can it be?

1. Explain what it means to have an average of 2.58 children in each family.

   _____

   _____

   _____

2. Milo also learns how "useful" averages can be: "For instance, if you didn't have any money at all, but you happened to be with four other people who had ten dollars apiece, then you'd each have a mean average of eight dollars." Can it be? Explain.

   _____

   _____

   _____

   _____

3. Are averages real? Look in a recent newspaper for any mention of an average. Describe what the average means in that situation.

   _____

   _____

   _____

   _____

   _____

   _____

From the *Arithmetic Teacher*, May 1993

Graphs of SKITTLES

LEVELS 4–5

Objective

To display and interpret descriptive statistics through sorting data and constructing frequency graphs. The students will also explore basic probability by calculating probabilities associated with selected subsamples and by using appropriate language to discuss outcomes.

Directions

1. Before beginning the activity, the teacher should purchase a large bag of snack-sized packages of SKITTLES. The teacher should also purchase five regular-sized bags of SKITTLES.

2. Reproduce "Completing the Histogram" and "Graphing Colors" and "Color Table" activity sheet for each student.

3. Give each student a snack-sized bag of SKITTLES.

4. Have students do a histogram (bar graph) and a scattergram using their snack-sized bag of SKITTLES and the information from the first column of the "Color Table" activity sheet and then compare their graphs. Have students decide which graph they believe is the easiest to interpret and why.

5. Put students into cooperative groups and give each group a regular-sized bag of SKITTLES and a new copy of "Completing the Histogram," "Graphing Colors," and the "Color Table" activity sheet.

6. Repeat step 4 as a group activity using a regular-sized bag of SKITTLES. Have students fill in the graphs in "Completing the Histogram" and "Graphing Colors."

7. Have the students complete the "Color Table" activity sheet and using their results, find the probabilities of picking the following colors of candy: (*a*) yellow, (*b*) green, (*c*) purple, (*d*) red or purple, and (*e*) orange or yellow. Have students compare these results with the data in their tables. Ask them to describe their observations orally.

8. Ask students to make predictions based on their group data:

a) If we put all the candies back into the bag and picked one piece of candy without looking, what color is it most likely to be? Why?

b) What color is least likely to be picked? Why?

c) Predict the color distribution for an unopened snack-sized bag and an unopened regular-sized bag of SKITTLES.

9. Have students use the data in their tables to make a pie chart using percents or decimals to represent their group data.

10. Have each group do an oral presentation of their results.

Family Activity

See "A Consuming Activity" on page 114.

Completing the Histogram
Complete the graph.

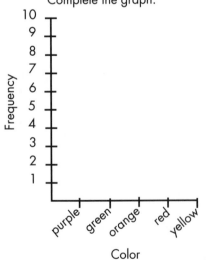

Graphing Colors
Complete the graph.

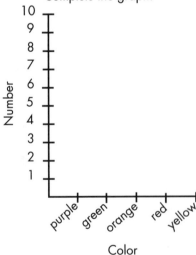

Prepared by Karen S. Norwood *and* Yvonne M. Coston
Edited by William R. Speer *and* Daniel J. Brahier

Name _____

Color Table

Group Data

Color	Number	Fractional part	Decimal part*	Percent
Purple				
Green				
Orange				
Red				
Yellow				
Red or purple				
Orange or yellow				
Total				

*Round to the nearest hundredth.

From the *Arithmetic Teacher*, April 1993

Preference Survey

LEVELS 6–8

Objectives

To explore measures of central tendencies, probabilities of events, and relationships among ranked data by computing averages, probabilities, and rank correlation coefficients

Directions

1. Reproduce a copy of the "Color Table" (on p. 29) and the "Preferred Colors" and "Correlation" activity sheet for each group.

2. Purchase a large bag of snack-sized packages of SKITTLES as well as five or six regular-sized bags of SKITTLES.

3. Set up cooperative learning groups of four or five students, and give each group a regular-sized bag of SKITTLES. Have each group sort and count their SKITTLES and fill in the "Color Table" sheet.

4. Have each group construct a different type of graph (e.g., pie, bar, scattergram, and so on) to display the color-table data from the group's SKITTLES pack.

   a) Have each group explain its graph to the class.

   b) Have the students decide, as a group, which graph appears to give the most information and why.

   c) Assign each group a color; have students find each group's number of SKITTLES of that color and use those data to find the mean, median, and mode for the number of that color of SKITTLES.

5. Have the students select their favorite color of SKITTLES, and have each group complete the "Preferred Colors" preference table with the class's totals. Have them calculate the probability that a new participant will select a particular color.

6. Before the groups begin the next activity, have each student choose one other

student in the group (they do not have to choose each other and the same individual can be chosen more than once). Once this is done, have the students fill in the top "Correlation" table with the group members' names and ratings. Have the students use each group member's name and ratings data and compare them with their own by constructing a scatterplot for each pair (e.g., if Jim, Bob, Sue, and Nate were a group, Jim would construct scatterplots for Jim-Bob, Jim-Sue, and Jim-Nate; for each color, each group member would do the same). An example might be a scatterplot based on the data in item 7.

7. Have each student correlate his or her color preferences with those of the student chosen in step 6. The students should compare their preferences by producing a Spearman rank correlation coefficient using calculators and the data from the bottom "Correlation" table.

  As an example, suppose Jim and Bob had the following results where d is the difference between the two sets of scores.

Jim	Bob	d
5	1	$5 - 1 = 4$
1	2	$1 - 2 = -1$
4	3	$4 - 3 = 1$
2	4	$2 - 4 = -2$
3	5	$3 - 5 = -2$

The formula would be

$$r = 1 - \frac{6(4^2 + (-1)^2 + 1^2 + (-2)^2 + (-2)^2)}{5(5^2 - 1)}$$

$$= 1 - \frac{6(16 + 1 + 1 + 4 + 4)}{5(24)} = 1 - \frac{6(26)}{5(24)}$$

$$= -0.3.$$

The correlation is not very strong; that is, the r value is not near +1 or –1. The negative value suggests a slight tendency for one set of data to be on the increase while the other is decreasing, and vice versa.

Prepared by Karen S. Norwood *and*
  Yvonne M. Coston
Edited by William R. Speer *and* Daniel J.
  Brahier

Applicable Standards

- **Algebra**
- **Statistics**
- **Probability**

a) Go through the activity sheet step by step with students.

b) Explain the meaning of correlation, and emphasize that a correlation rating can range from –1 to +1. Also, explain the difference between a negative and a positive correlation. A value close to 1 suggests that the trend in two sets of scores is the same, either rising together or falling together. A value close to –1 suggests that as one group of scores increases the other group decreases, or vice versa.

c) Students may wish to choose another student with whom to test the relationship between their ratings.

d) Have students interpret results from the "Correlation" tables.

8. Give each group a snack-sized bag of SKITTLES, and ask the students to construct snack-sized bags on the basis of the proportions from the regular-sized bag.

   a) How many snack-sized bags can be made from a regular-sized bag?

   b) Would it be cheaper to buy a bag of snack-sized packages of SKITTLES or buy a few regular-sized bags of SKITTLES and make snack-sized bags so that each student would have the equivalent of a snack-sized bag of SKITTLES?

Family Activity

See "A Consuming Activity" on page 114.

Name _____

Preferred Colors

Preference Table

Use the class totals for favorite colors to complete the table at the right.

If you were the manufacturer of SKITTLES, how might you use the data in the preference table?

Color	Number	Percent
Purple		
Green		
Orange		
Red		
Yellow		
Total		

Correlation

Are you like the rest of the people in your group? Each member of your group should rate the colors of SKITTLES from 1 (favorite) to 5 (least favorite). Before rating the colors, circle the name of one person in the group whose ratings you are going to rank correlate with your own ratings.

Your Group Members' Names and Ratings

	Color	Your name	Name 2	Name 3	Name 4
Rating	Purple				
	Green				
	Orange				
	Red				
	Yellow				

How do your ratings compare? The Spearman rank correlation can be used to test the strength of the relationship between your ratings and another student's ratings. Here is the rank-correlation formula:

$$r = 1 - \frac{6\Sigma d^2}{n(n^2 - 1)}$$

In the formula, r = correlation coefficient; d = the difference between the two ratings; Σ = the Greek letter sigma, a mathematical symbol for sum; n = the number of items that were ranked; and 6 = a constant in the formula.

Copy in the table below the two columns of pertinent data from the foregoing table.

	Color	Your data	Other students' data	d	d^2
Rating	Purple				
	Green				
	Orange				
	Red				
	Yellow				

The sum of all your $d^2 = \Sigma d^2 =$ _____ . $n =$ _____ .

Insert the appropriate numbers in the formula and solve: $r = 1 - \dfrac{6\ \boxed{}}{\boxed{}(\boxed{} - 1)} =$ ____

From the *Arithmetic Teacher*, April 1993

We Flip over Art

LEVELS 7–8

Background

Although the geometric thinking of students in the middle grades should be maturing toward the formal deductive thinking needed for high school geometry, reasoning skills and concepts associated with lower levels should be reviewed and consolidated. In the primary grades, students identify, extend, and create patterns. As students progress through the grades, patterning and the process of identifying connecting characteristics must be incorporated into a wide range of classroom activities. In the upper grades, patterning can lend opportunities to investigate transformational geometry; build spatial skills, which are useful in high school geometry; and connect mathematics to art through developing visual patterns.

Objective

To explore such geometric transformations as flips and turns and their uses in developing patterns

Directions

1. Discuss such geometric transformations as flips (reflection), slides (translation), and turns (rotation). For example, cut a large block capital letter, such as an **F**, out of poster board. Demonstrate the resulting appearance of the letter as it is flipped, or reflected, about a line (**Ⅎ**); slid, or translated, along a line (**F**); and turned, or rotated, about a point (**ʌ**). When discussing flips, be certain to include flips across both horizontal and vertical lines and one-half and one-fourth turns.

2. Hand out copies of the "We Flip over Art" activity page.

3. Discuss the examples at the top of the activity page with the class as a group. Illustrate the result of each of the five defined moves. Two identical transparencies with the figure imprinted can be used to show the starting configuration and the move or moves necessary to arrive at the ending configuration.

4. Have the students complete questions 1 and 2, discuss their conclusions as a class, and demonstrate their conclusions.

5. Ask the students to work individually or in pairs on questions 3 and 4. When they are finished, have the students demonstrate their results.

6. Question 5 can be used as an independent or small-group project.

Answers

1. Right or left flips, up or down flips, one-fourth turns right or left

2. Duplicate and one-half turns right or left

3. a)   b)   c)   d)   e)

4. Duplicate and one-half turns right or left

5.

Prepared by Virginia Usnick, Phyllis Knerl Miller, *and* Danna Stonecipher
Edited by William R. Speer *and* Daniel J. Brahier

Applicable Standards

- **Reasoning**
- **Patterns and Functions**
- **Geometry**

Extensions

1. Create a design within a square so that flipping right or left results in a duplicate of the original but flipping up or down does not.

2. Have students investigate and analyze border patterns on pottery.

3. Investigate the use of transformational geometry in quilt patterns.

4. Have the students describe the conditions necessary for a geometric figure to look the same after being flipped as it did before.

Name _____

We Flip over Art

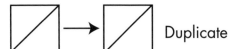 Duplicate

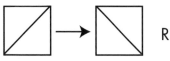 Right or left flip

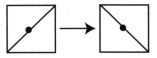 One-fourth turn right or left

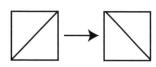 Up or down flip

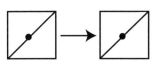 One-half turn right or left

1. Which moves change to ? _____

2. Which moves seem to leave the design unchanged? _____

3. Complete the pictures to show the result of the described action.

Start with   Start with

a) 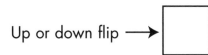 Duplicate ⟶ ☐

b) Right or left flip ⟶ ☐

c) Up or down flip ⟶ ☐

d) One-fourth turn right or left ⟶ ☐

e) 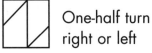 One-half turn right or left ⟶ ☐

4. Which of the moves described seem to leave the design unchanged? _____

5. Start with

Move from square to square by making one-fourth turns to the right.

From the *Arithmetic Teacher*, March 1993

Testing the Strength of Paper Tubes

LEVELS 5–6

Objectives

To develop measurement skills, as well as to collect, record, organize, and analyze data generated through hands-on explorations

Directions

1. Before this session, assemble materials to make tubes; this might include one or two reams of copy paper, scissors, cellophane tape, and white glue. For strength tests, collect uniform weights, such as spelling books, metal washers, or gram and centimeter cubes. You will also need paper cups, string, and large paper clips to suspend the weights from the tubes during the second series of tests. A balance with some standardized weights can be used to compare results across groups.

2. Begin by asking your class, "Does this piece of paper have much strength?" Allow time for comments. "What do we mean by strength? What is a strong person? How might we define a strong piece of paper?" Allow time for students to struggle with this definition and to come to some agreement. Suggest to students that they may soon be surprised at how strong they can make a piece of paper.

3. Have each student try to make a piece of paper strong enough to support some weight, such as a quarter, a pencil, or a box of crayons. Ask students to work in small groups to explore the problem briefly. Encourage them to make connections with structures in their environments. Draw or write some of the principles students discover on the chalkboard. These principles will generally involve either folding or rolling the paper.

4. Challenge students to make a tube of paper that will support weight. They might begin by attempting to support a relatively light object. Then expand the search to support as much weight as possible. Divide students into small teams for the remainder of the session. They may keep track of their information on the activity sheet.

Ask students to test the weight-bearing capacity of tubes when they are horizontal and bridging an 8-inch space (see fig. 1). Groups can collect data to see whether strength is altered under different conditions, such as changing the length of a tube, changing the circumference, or changing the thickness of the tube wall.

To make a tube of a certain circumference, take a piece of yarn a little larger than the desired circumference and tie it to make a closed curve. When the yarn is placed around an untaped tube of paper, the paper will uncurl to that circumference and can then be taped.

5. When groups of students have collected and recorded some data, ask them to make some conjectures about the diameter of a paper tube that supports maximal weight. Does it seem to be related to the length of the paper tube? Under what conditions is the tube the strongest? Is general agreement found as to those conditions? What further experiments could students do to test these conjectures?

Extensions

See whether joined tubes support much more weight than single tubes. If a single tube can support 35 grams, can three tubes fastened together support 3×35 grams? Can they support more? You will need ten or twelve dozen drinking straws, rubber bands to fasten them together, and perhaps string. First, test a drinking straw to see how much weight it can support in horizontal and vertical positions. Next, bundle five more straws, for a total of six, and see how much weight the sheaf then supports. Is it simply five or six times more? Does the amount increase by even more? If you make a graph to show these results, does it demonstrate a predictable pattern?

When straws are linked in different ways, they may have different weight-bearing characteristics. When bundles of tubes are attached, how much does the weight-bearing capacity increase? Can students find ways of making bundles of straws longer than the straws themselves? Does length seem to make a difference in weight-bearing capacity?

Prepared by Rebecca B. Corwin
Edited by Daniel J. Brahier *and* William R. Speer

Applicable Standards

- **Communication**
- **Reasoning**
- **Statistics**
- **Measurement**

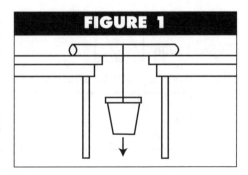

FIGURE 1

Name _____

Testing the Strength of Paper Tubes

Your group will make paper tubes, place them between desks, and hang a container from each tube to see how much weight it will hold.

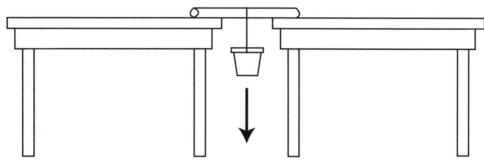

1. Make six paper tubes that have different dimensions. With your group, find ways to test those tubes until they fail. Keep track of how much weight each tube supports before it collapses. Record the data for each tube that you make and test.

Length of tube	Circumference of tube	Maximum weight supported

2. What makes a tube strong? Talk over this question with your group members and record your ideas here. _____

_____

_____

3. Using the information you got from your experiments and your group discussion, make one piece of paper hold as much weight as possible. Record your results here, and compare with others in the class.

Length of tube	Circumference of tube	Maximum weight supported

From the *Arithmetic Teacher*, February 1993

IDEAS

Spanning to the Max!

LEVELS 7–8

Objectives

To experiment with a tightly constrained design problem; to develop and modify designs and test their strength. Information gained from testing leads to further analysis, redesign, and refinement of previous designs to optimize performance by manipulating variables.

Materials

A ream of copy paper, ten or twelve containers of white glue, rulers, yardsticks, and good scissors

Directions

1. Tell students that part of the culture of architecture is competing to solve design problems. Architects are often challenged to produce their best designs under pressure, with the understanding that learning occurs during such challenges. Today your students will work individually or in pairs to respond to a difficult challenge.

2. Place two student desks so that they are 2 feet apart. Take one piece of 8 1/2-inch-by-11-inch paper and tell students that they are to experiment making the paper strong enough to bridge the 2-foot space. They may cut, fold, and glue, but the bridge they construct must be self-standing. If they insist it's impossible, suggest that a bridge *can* be constructed that spans more than 8 feet and supports a quarter in the center.

3. As students begin to work on the problem, encourage them to share ideas. Some students may want to find pictures so that they can think about what bridges look like or how they are

constructed. Others may set right to work. Allow students to start over as often as they like. Remind them they may use only one piece of 8 1/2-inch-by-11-inch paper in each attempt.

4. As some successful design strategies develop, encourage students to modify their ideas to explore the limits of the problem. You may want to have a short class meeting to share some observations about successful designs.

5. As a next phase, encourage students to expand the problem by looking for the longest bridge or the tallest structure they can make. The principles are similar, although the details are different.

6. After an appropriate amount of working time, ask students to analyze the most successful attempts. What is the longest distance spanned so far? What do the longest designs have in common? What is similar and what is different about the ways they are designed? Students may see that some general patterns seem to apply to many of the successful designs. Ask if they can test their conjecture, whether a counterexample is found among the bridges in the class, and how the conjecture rose from looking at the class's designs.

7. Finally, ask students to use the activity sheet to record these designs and to write about their experiences in doing the problem. Remind them that writing in mathematics is very important but sometimes hard to do. Circulate as they are writing, asking questions that push students to think further about what they have done and to reflect on their experiences.

Applicable Standards

- **Problem Solving**
- **Communication**
- **Connections**
- **Measurement**

Extensions

Challenge students to make the strongest 2-foot bridge they can by testing structures with weights until they fail, and encourage students to predict which they think are the most effective designs. Extract the principles they believe will lead to the greatest strength.

Answers

Here are three ways to create the length and strength required for this kind of structure:

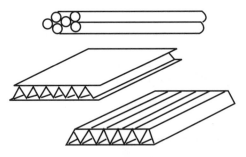

- Folding and sandwiching between strips of paper will create a structure resembling corrugated cardboard.
- Cutting strips that are folded into triangular prisms and linked together.
- Making small tubes of paper that are glued together or one tube that spans the distance on its own.

Prepared by Rebecca B. Corwin
Edited by Daniel J. Brahier *and* William R. Speer

Name _____

Spanning to the Max!

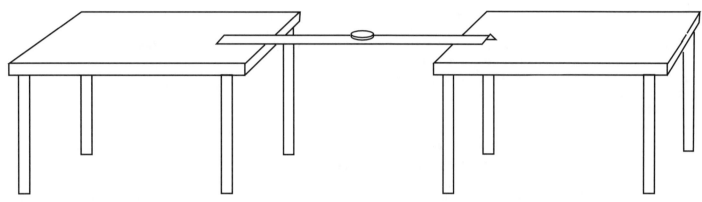

1. After your class has made some successful bridges from paper, sketch your own design and one or two of the others in the space below so that you will have a record of them.

2. What were your ideas as you worked on building your bridge? What were some of the important things you tried? _____

_____

_____

3. What advice would you give a fifth grader about making a strong bridge from one piece of paper? _____

_____

_____

_____

_____

From the *Arithmetic Teacher*, February 1993

Super Bowl Scores

LEVELS 4–6

Objective

To determine different numerical arrangements that, when added, represent a given amount. This investigation will lead to a discussion of multiples and combinations of multiples.

Directions

1. Reproduce a copy of the activity sheet for each student.

2. Read the introductory information to the students. Discuss with the class the fact that for a football team to have a certain number of points, only certain combinations of scores can be made. For example, for a team to have 5 points, they would have to have made one field goal and one safety. Some students may need to be told the meaning of a safety and have a brief review of the way football is scored.

3. Encourage the students to explore and develop as many possibilities as they can generate. The "bar-number-line" approach suggested on the activity page can be used to help them explore possibilities. You might consider using Unifix or Multilink cubes to represent points. If, for example, red cubes stand for 1 point, two green cubes stand for 2 points, three blue cubes stand for 3 points, and six white cubes stand for 6 points, then 10 points could be represented by any "train" of cubes shown in figure 1.

Answers

1. Buffalo needed 14 additional points to win the game. Therefore, they needed at least one of the following combinations of touchdowns, extra points, and field goals:

- Two touchdowns with extra points
- One touchdown with an extra point and three field goals

Prepared by J. David Keller
Edited by Daniel J. Brahier *and* William R. Speer

- One touchdown without converting the extra point and three field goals
- Five field goals

2. A total of 6 points would need to be scored, which could occur in three ways: two field goals, one touchdown without the extra point, or three safeties.

3. Several answers are possible depending on the number of missed conversions of extra points. Six ways are possible for the Buffalo Bills:

- Three touchdowns with extra points and one field goal
- Four touchdowns with no extra points
- Eight field goals
- Three touchdowns, no extra points, and two field goals
- Two touchdowns, no extra points, and four field goals
- One touchdown, no extra point, and six field goals

Seven ways are possible for the Washington Redskins:

- Five touchdowns with four extra points and one field goal
- Five touchdowns with one extra point and two field goals
- Four touchdowns with all extra points and three field goals
- Four touchdowns with one extra point and four field goals
- Three touchdowns with one extra point and six field goals
- Two touchdowns with one extra point and eight field goals
- One touchdown with no extra points and ten field goals

4. Along with the 155 plays from the line of scrimmage, the game would have involved 13 kickoffs (2 to begin the halves, 7 after the touchdowns, 4 after field goals), 4 field goals, and 7 extra points, as well as any missed field-goal attempts and punts. Therefore, the footballs would have been used more than 175 times. Each football would have been used for 3 or 4 plays (since the computed average is greater than 3.7).

Extensions

1. Have students make a bar graph for Super Bowl XXVII. Ask them to develop questions related to the possible scores of the game.

2. Ask students to describe the different combinations of gains that a team can use to make a first down in four downs or fewer. For example, they can make the first down in one play, or they can make 9 yards in one play and 1 yard in the second, or they can make 8 yards in one play and 2 yards in the second, and so forth. You may want to discuss the possibility of losses, penalties, and nonintegral gains.

FIGURE 1

G	G	G	G	G
B		B		G		G
B			W		R
W			G		G

(or the same in some other order)

(or the same in WRB order)

(or the same in some other order)

Super Bowl Scores

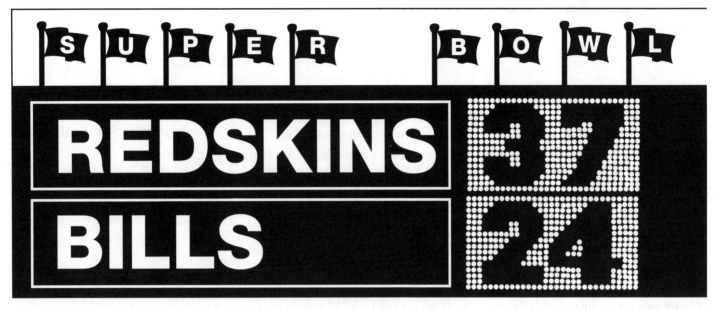

In the National Football League, teams score 3 points for a field goal, 2 points for a safety, 6 points for a touchdown, and 1 point for an extra point. The extra point can be scored only after a touchdown.

In 1992, the Washington Redskins beat the Buffalo Bills by the score of 37 to 24. Washington scored its points by making four touchdowns and three field goals. Buffalo scored three touchdowns and one field goal. Both teams made all their extra points. The bar graph below shows the scoring for each team.

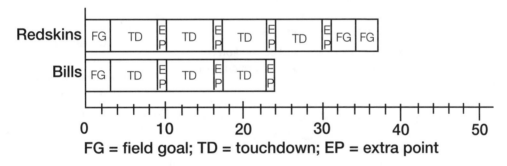

FG = field goal; TD = touchdown; EP = extra point

1. How many additional touchdowns (with extra points) and/or field goals would Buffalo need to have scored to win the game? _____

2. The record for most total points in a Super Bowl is 66, set in 1977 when the Pittsburgh Steelers beat the Dallas Cowboys 35 to 31. What is the minimum number of additional points Washington and Buffalo would need to have scored to break the record? _____ In how many ways could exactly this number of points have been scored?_____

3. If neither the Redskins nor the Bills had had a safety, how could the teams have ended with the same score (37 to 24) by scoring different combinations of touchdowns and field goals?_____

4. In Super Bowl XXVI, forty-eight footballs were used for the game. Washington made 73 plays from the line of scrimmage. Buffalo made 82. If the referees tried to use each football an equal number of times, what is the average number of plays for which each football was used? _____

From the *Arithmetic Teacher*, January 1993

IDEAS

Football Finances

LEVELS 7–8

Background

In this activity, students analyze pictures of football stands to make estimates related to the attendance at the Super Bowl. The students will realize that estimates must, at times, be made with little background information and that a range of answers might be correct. Students also make estimates about the television audience.

Objective

To estimate the number representing a large group on the basis of pictures and from other limited information.

Directions

1. Reproduce a copy of the activity page for each student.

2. Have the students read the introductory information and examine the pictures.

3. Discuss the pictures with the students and have them identify techniques that they can use to make the best estimates possible. Such techniques might include these:

- How many people can sit on benches 10 yards long?

- Survey people about the number of hot dogs they eat at a football game.

4. Have students make their estimates on the information that is available.

5. Have students identify factors that will make it difficult for their estimates to be as accurate as they would like them to be.

Answers

1. Answers will vary. Students should describe a strategy used to obtain their answer. For example, the number of people in the close-up picture of the crowd is about YY people. This number is about (fraction) of the people in one section of the stands, and the stadium has XX sections in all.

2. Answers will vary according to survey information and guesses made.

3. Answers will vary according to the survey information and guesses made.

4. Answers will vary ($18 025 000 on the basis of the Rose Bowl capacity of 103 000 people).

5. Answers will vary. Some factors include teams participating, weather, time of the game, closeness of the game as it progresses, and the like.

6. Answers will vary. Be certain to hold a discussion on ways in which one might arrive at an answer to such a

Applicable Standards

- **Communication**
- **Reasoning**
- **Connections**
- **Computation and Estimation**

question.

7. Answers will vary. Be certain to hold a discussion on ways in which one might arrive at an answer to such a question.

8. Answers will be based on data collected during the game.

Extensions

1. Have students identify variables (e.g., temperature at the stadium) that would affect the actual results.

2. Have students gather information after the football game is over to see how close their estimates are.

3. Have students make estimates of the number of souvenirs (e.g., pennants, sweatshirts, and hats) that will be purchased.

Prepared by J. David Keller
Edited by Daniel J. Brahier *and* William R. Speer

Football Finances

Using the pictures above, give your best estimates for questions 1–4 below.

1. How many people are attending the game? _____
   Explain how you arrived at your estimate. _____
   _____
   _____
   _____

2. How many hot dogs will be eaten at the stadium? _____
   If each hot dog weighs 2 ounces, how many pounds of hot dogs will be eaten? _____

3. At the football stadium, how many gallons of soft drinks will be drunk? _____

4. Tickets for the Super Bowl cost approximately $175 each. What is the total value of all the tickets sold for the game?
   _____

5. Estimators predict that 112 million people in the United States will watch the game on television at Super Bowl parties, large and small. What factors will influence how many

people actually watch the game? _____
   _____
   _____
   _____
   _____

6. Assuming that 112 million people do watch the game, how many Super Bowl parties do you think will be held throughout the United States?_____

7. How many bags of potato chips will be eaten at the Super Bowl parties? _____

8. How many commercials will run on television during the game? _____

9. If each 30-second advertisement costs $800 000, how much will the television network be paid to broadcast advertising during the football game? _____

From the *Arithmetic Teacher*, January 1993

IDEAS

Rock 'r Rap

LEVELS 5–6

Background

Individuals of all ages can enjoy music, but their preferences for a particular type of music often differ. Age may be the dominant factor, but gender may also play a significant role. Whether a student has an older sibling and is thus exposed to other types or music may affect his or her preferences.

Objective

To define a problem and ask a well-defined question that could be answered by means of data collection, to conduct a survey and display the data by multiple methods, and to interpret bar graphs in writing

Directions

1. Ask the students what kind of music they like or to what music they like to listen. If they give the names of some particular singers rather than types of music, the subject of the survey can be singers of different types or you can explain that the singers they have mentioned are folk singers, blues singers, soul singers, or singers of other types of music. Try to get opinions from several of the students.

2. Discuss with students questions 1 and 2 on the activity sheet. Be certain that the benefits of conducting a survey are brought out in the discussion.

3. Decide as a class whether the survey will be on particular singers or on types of music. Compile a list of either types of music that have been mentioned (e.g., rock 'n' roll, rhythm and blues, rap, folk rock, reggae, soul, Motown, country and western, hard rock, heavy metal) or performers of music (e.g., Michael Jackson, Elvis Presley, Muddy Waters, Paul Simon, Hammer, Loretta Lynn, Phil Collins). Limit the number of choices to four with a fifth category including "others." To preserve ano-

nymity and reduce the chances that a particular student will influence others, have each student record his or her preference on a small piece of paper. After collecting and shuffling the papers, have some students record the results on a tally chart at the chalkboard. The rest of the students should fill in the activity sheet with this information.

4. Display the data in the bar graph in problem 4 on the activity sheet.

5. Ask the students if they think that girls' and boys' preferences in music (or musicians) differ. Fill out the bar graph in problem 5 on the activity page. Ask the students to determine from the bar graph whether boys' and girls' preferences differ.

6. Discuss the magnitude of this class's range of preferences in music or musicians. Point out the chart at the bottom of the activity sheet that shows music preferences and number of audiotapes and CDs (compact discs) owned by a hypothetical group of students. On the basis of the data in the chart, discuss the probable preferences of a "typical" student in the class, "Marge," for each category. Note that a discussion of the uses of the mean, median, and mode can arise.

7. Ask the students whether they think that all opinions are represented in their class. Ask how one might find out the opinions of other people. (Go to a record store and find out what types of cassette tapes, CDs, etc., are popular; ask other people what types or music they like.)

8. Ask the students if they would expect that certain groups of people have very different preferences from those of their class. Why? What factors might influence a person's musical preference? (Age, number of older siblings, interest in athletics, and many other factors)

Answers

Answers will vary. For question 7, however, you might bring out the value of

Applicable Standards

- **Communication**
- **Statistics**

using different methods to determine Marge's probable music preference. Using the mode (most common) is one way to determine the probable number of tapes and CDs owned (9), but another appropriate value, the mean (arithmetic average), yields a different answer (11). The use of the median (middle of a ranked list) yields still another possible answer (10).

Extensions

1. Have the students survey their parents' preferences in music and construct a bar graph contrasting the adults' preferences with the students' preferences. Have them write a report on whether differences in age seem to play a more significant role than differences in gender.

2. Have the students predict whether having one or more older siblings influences music preferences. Have them decide who to survey and how to carry out the survey. Have them construct tally charts and bar graphs. Then have them write their interpretations of the bar graphs.

3. Compare the survey results of this class with those of other classes at other grade levels in the school. Begin by dividing the class into groups of five, then have each group compose a letter to another class. The letter must contain an explanation of the subject of the survey and a tally chart that the surveyed class must fill in. When the survey results are returned, each group should display the results in a bar graph. Discuss how information from all groups could be combined.

Family activity

See "Station to Station" on page 116.

Prepared by Barbara E. Moses *and* Linda Proudfit
Edited by Daniel J. Brahier *and* William R. Speer

Rock 'r Rap

1. What type of music do you think is the most popular type in your class? _____

2. How could you check your guess? _____

_____

3. Fill in the tally chart below.

	Music or musician	(Tally marks)	Number
Music preferences	A. _____		
(or musician preferences)	B. _____		
	C. _____		
	D. _____		
	E. Other		

4. Make a bar graph displaying the results:

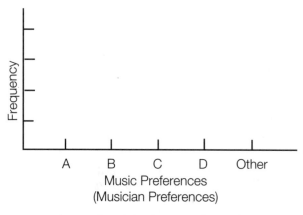

5. Make a bar graph displaying boys' and girls' preferences separately:

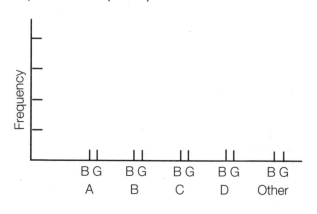

6. Interpret the results of the bar graph you have just constructed. _____

_____

7. Marge is a new student who will be joining the class. If Marge is a "typical student," use the data in the chart below to predict Marge's preferences. How did you decide what to put in each category?

Student	Music preference	Number of musical audiotapes and CDs owned
Tom	Rock	8
Rena	Country	11
Anna	Motown	9
Natasha	Rock	9
Willie	Soul	18
Tessa	Rock	12
Carl	Country	10

From the *Arithmetic Teacher*, December 1992

IDEAS

What Should We Eat?

LEVELS 5–6

Background

People make decisions all the time—What should I wear? Where should I go? Whom shall I invite to go with me? How much will it cost? Since we make so many decisions, we would be well advised to devote more attention to doing it wisely.

Decision making is similar to the election process in that both involve the dynamics of choice. Choice creates a dilemma—how do we choose? The decisions we make may be "informed" decisions based on related information or they may be based on hunches or attitudes. Sometimes we make important decisions on the basis of information that isn't important.

In this activity, students examine factors involved in a decision about what the cafeteria should serve for the school's open house. The students are given information about the preferences of a hypothetical class and asked to help make a decision. The students analyze information using various strategies, each of which leads to a different conclusion.

Objective

To identify the relative importance of the factors involved in a decision and to justify the reasoning for specific decisions.

Directions

1. Before distributing the activity sheet, outline the problem at the top of the page. Set the task as an authentic problem that the class can help solve.

2. Seek possible methods of deciding what to serve. Ask, "What method would you suggest to help decide on the main dish?" Lead students to suggest such options as "Let the teacher decide," "Find out what everyone likes," "Take a vote," and "Have several

Prepared by Daniel J. Brahier, Anne F. Brahier, *and* William R. Speer

Edited by Daniel J. Brahier *and* William R. Speer

different foods available." Explain that any of these methods might be acceptable in certain situations.

3. Ask the students to take into consideration the conditions of question 1 on the activity sheet and then revise their thinking. This restriction should limit the methods of solution to those that yield one choice. Examples include "Let the teacher decide," "Let _____ decide because today is his or her birthday," and so on. Lead the discussion toward the notion of taking a vote. Once again, any method that results in a single solution might be acceptable, depending on the circumstances.

4. Have the students use the data to complete question 2 and then discuss their responses. Since most voted for hamburgers, should we recommend that hamburgers be the food served in the cafeteria? Point out that one way to decide is on the basis of the principle that a plurality ("most votes") wins.

5. Next, use the answers to question 3 to focus students' attention on the fact that more people didn't vote for hamburgers than did. We cannot yet make a decision on the basis of majority rule, since no choice was selected by more than half the class. The students or the teacher might suggest eliminating the food with the fewest votes and then voting again, using only the top two choices.

6. As the students explore the information in question 4 on the activity sheet, mention the notion of rank ordering. Students should determine that hamburgers get a total of 51 points (12×1 point + 10×3 points + 3×3 points); hot dogs get a total of 52 points (12×3 points + 10×1 point + 3×2 points); and fish sticks get a total of 47 points (12×2 points + 10×2 points + 3×1 point). Under this system of ranking, the food with the least point total "wins."

7. For question 5, teachers might want to encourage the students to devise methods of decision that yield the choice of hot dogs. Encourage diver-

gent thought. No single answer or single method is correct.

Answers

1. Answers will vary (see step 2 under directions).

2. Hamburgers

3. 12; 13; Answers will vary.

4. This method suggests that fish sticks are the most acceptable alternative (see step 6 under directions).

5. Answers will vary. One approach that might lead to the choice of hot dogs is a runoff between the two top vote getters. Hot dogs would win if the three sway votes from fish sticks went to hot dogs. Be certain that students recognize that different conclusions can be arrived at on the basis of the same information.

Extensions

1. Compare the procedure of dropping the food with the fewest votes and then voting on the remaining choices with the procedure commonly used in primary elections. Is it possible that we might drop the candidate who would be the best compromise for all concerned?

2. Another way to explore the data in this situation is to use percent. Note that only 12 percent favored fish sticks, but 100 percent picked them first or second. Forty-eight percent chose hamburgers first, but 52 percent picked them last.

Family Activity

See "Exploring Election Calendar Dates" on page 118.

Applicable Standards

- **Connections**
- **Number and Number Relationships**
- **Computation and Estimation**

Name _____

What Should We Eat?

The students in Mr. Jona's class have been asked to help the cafeteria decide what food to serve for lunch for the school's open house. The school expects a large crowd and wants to offer food that people will enjoy.

1. If the school principal tells you that the class has to agree on just one choice, how can you decide which it will be?

_____

2. The students in the class voted on their favorites, with the following results:

Favorite food	Number of students
Hamburgers	12
Hot dogs	10
Fish sticks	3

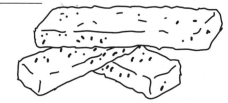

On the basis of this information, which choice of food did more people want served in the cafeteria?

3. Look at the chart in question 2. How many people wanted hamburgers?_____ How many people didn't want hamburgers? _____ Since more people didn't want hamburgers than did, describe another way to use the information in the chart to help decide on the food to be served. _____

_____

4. The students were asked to order their preferences from the three choices found in the charts. When they did, they got these results:

The 12 who liked hamburgers best _____   The 3 who liked fish sticks best _____

chose fish sticks second _____   chose hot dogs second _____

and hot dogs last. _____   and hamburgers last. _____

The 10 who liked hot dogs best _____

chose fish sticks second _____

and hamburgers last. _____

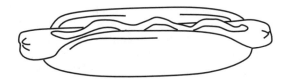

For each group of students, give the first choice a point value of 1, second choice a value of 2, and third choice a value of 3. Multiply the point value by the number of students in that group. To determine the ranking, find the total points for each food. What seems to be the best choice to serve in the cafeteria if we use this method to determine the favorite of the class? _____

5. What other ways can you think of to help the class decide? Which do you think would be the best way?_____

_____

Do you think that only one right way exists? _____ Why?_____

_____

From the *Arithmetic Teacher*, November 1992

Presidential Photo Finishes

LEVELS 7–8

Objectives

To work with percents, to round numbers, to estimate, and to perform the basic operations on a calculator for analysis of statistical data. The activity sheet naturally connects mathematics and social studies.

Directions

1. Begin with a discussion of the Electoral College. As an example, use a student-council election in an elementary school that has one class at each grade level, K–6. Seven votes would be cast—one for each grade level. A candidate who receives a majority of the votes in four of the seven classes would get elected, regardless of the total popular vote. Table 1 shows how candidate I. M. Close might get the most votes in the school but lose because candidate N. O. Cigar won in four classes out of seven (the greatest "electoral" vote). The winning totals in each class are underscored.

Explain that to make the election more nearly fair, classes with more students would have to be given more weight than those with fewer students. For example, a class that has thirty students would get two "electoral" votes and one with fifteen students would get only one.

2. Distribute an activity sheet to each student. Divide students into teams of from two to four students to complete the activity sheet with a calculator.

3. Set the stage using the election of 1824. The candidates were John Quincy Adams, Andrew Jackson, William Harris Crawford, and Henry Clay. The voting results and follow-up questions are on the activity page. After students complete this section, discuss the answers with the class. The strong finish of the third and fourth candidates created a unique situation. Adams lost

Prepared by Daniel J. Brahier, Anne F. Brahier, *and* William R. Speer
Edited by Daniel J. Brahier *and* William R. Speer

in the popular vote and took second place initially, but in the vote by the House, he won the election.

4. Discuss the election of 1876, in which Samuel Tilden ran against Rutherford B. Hayes. The three other candidates (Cooper, Smith, and Walker) collectively received just over 1 percent of the vote. When students have completed the questions about this election on the activity sheet, discuss the answers as a class.

5. On 3 November 1948, the *Chicago Daily Tribune* carried the headline "Dewey Defeats Truman." However, the headline was wrong—the presidential race was simply too close to call, and the press had called it wrong. Have students complete the final section of the activity sheet, then discuss the results.

Answers

1. A total of 362 744 people voted.

2. Adams received 32 percent of the popular vote, and Jackson received 42 percent.

3. Crawford received the fewest popular votes, but Clay received the fewest electoral votes because Crawford won a couple of large states (specifically, he won 24 of his 41 electoral votes in Virginia).

4. The total of the second- and third-place electoral votes is 125, more than the first-place finish of 99 electoral votes.

5. John Quincy Adams won the election in the vote by the House because states that had originally chosen Clay voted for Adams after Clay was withdrawn from consideration. Adams is the only president ever chosen by the House of Representatives.

6. Tilden received 51 percent of the popular vote (4 287 670 out of 8 418 529). But he lost the election because he received one fewer electoral vote than Hayes.

Applicable Standards

- **Connections**
- **Number and Number Relationships**
- **Computation and Estimation**

7. If 464 voters in Florida had changed their minds, the final vote count would have been 23 386 for Hayes and 23 387 for Tilden. In this event, Tilden would have received the four electoral votes from Florida. The final count would have been Hayes, 181 (185 – 4 from Florida) and Tilden, 188 (184 + 4 from Florida), and Tilden would have won the election!

8. A total of 48 401 129 voters cast ballots in the 1948 election. Dividing this number by 0.511 (51.1%) yields approximately 94 720 000 eligible voters in 1948.

9. Harry Truman received 57 percent of the electoral votes but just under 50 percent of the popular vote.

10. If the 50 electoral votes from these two states had been shifted, Truman would have ended up with 253 (303—50) and Dewey would have had 239 (189 + 50), with Thurmond carrying 39 electoral votes. Those 39 votes would have represented a balance of power, since Dewey's 239 plus the other 39 could have defeated Truman. Therefore, the election would have been sent to the House of Representatives to determine the outcome.

Family activity

See "Exploring Election Calendar Dates" on page 118.

TABLE 1								
Class Votes								Total
Candidate	K	1	2	3	4	5	6	popular vote
N. O. Cigar	8	9	_18_	_16_	7	9	_19_	86
I. M. Close	_12_	_11_	2	4	_13_	_11_	1	54

Presidential Photo Finishes

★ ★ ★ ★ ★ ★ ★ ★

In the presidential election of 1824, the candidates received the following numbers of votes:

Candidate	Popular vote	Electoral votes
John Quincy Adams	115 696	84
Andrew Jackson	152 933	99
William Harris Crawford	46 979	41
Henry Clay	47 136	37

1. How many people voted in the 1824 election? _____

2. What percent of the popular vote did Adams receive? _____ Jackson? _____ (Round answers to the nearest whole percent.)

3. Which candidate received the fewest popular votes? _____

   Did he also receive the fewest electoral votes? _____

   Explain why this outcome might have happened. _____

   _____

4. What is the total number of electoral votes received by the second- and third-place finishers? _____

   Is this total greater than the number of electoral votes received by the first-place finisher? _____

5. Because no candidate received a majority of electoral votes, the Electoral College decided that no clear-cut winner of the election could be determined. They asked the House of Representatives to choose between the three top electoral-vote winners. When the House voted, Jackson carried seven states, Adams carried thirteen states, and Crawford carried four states. Use library resources to find out the final winner of the election. _____

   What happened that allowed him to win the election? __

   _____

★ ★ ★ ★ ★ ★ ★ ★

In the presidential election of 1876, the vote totals were as follows:

Candidate	Popular vote	Electoral votes
Rutherford B. Hayes	4 035 924	185
Samuel J. Tilden	4 287 670	184
Other three candidates	94 935	0

6. Which candidate received the majority of the popular vote? _____

   What percent of the total popular votes cast did he receive? _____ Did he win the election? _____
   Explain. _____

7. In Florida, Hayes defeated Tilden to win the state's 4 electoral votes by receiving 23 849 votes to Tilden's 22 923. How many people would have had to change their votes in Florida for Tilden to have won the state?

   Explain your answer. _____

   If Tilden had won in Florida, what would have been the final electoral-vote count for Hayes and Tilden?_____

   Who would have won the election? _____

★ ★ ★ ★ ★ ★ ★ ★

In the presidential election of 1948, the vote totals were as follows:

Candidate	Popular vote	Electoral votes
Harry S. Truman	24 104 030	303
Thomas E. Dewey	21 971 004	189
James Thurmond	1 169 032	39
Henry A. Wallace	1 157 063	0

8. How many people altogether voted in the election?

   _____

   Records show that 51.1 percent of the eligible voters actually voted in the election. Approximately how many citizens were eligible to vote in 1948?_____

9. What percent of the popular vote did Harry Truman get? _____ What percent of the electoral votes did he receive? _____

10. Records show that if 12 487 voters in California and Ohio had voted for Dewey instead of Truman, those two states' electoral votes would have been cast for Dewey. If California and Ohio each carried 25 electoral votes, explain how the election results would have changed. _____

    _____

    _____

From the *Arithmetic Teacher*, November 1992

Lewis and Clark and Me

LEVELS 4–6

Background

In this activity, students read a story of an imaginary trip and then select a graph that represents that story. Students are also given a line graph representing the relation of time and distance on Lewis and Clark's expedition through the Louisiana Purchase. On the basis of the graph, the students write a story about what may have happened on this journey.

Meriwether Lewis and William Clark set out from Saint Louis, Missouri, on 14 May 1804 to explore the northwestern part of the Louisiana Purchase. They began their journey by boat, sailing up the Missouri River. By late September 1804, they had reached what is now known as North Dakota, where they wintered for five months. During August 1805, they were in what is now western Montana. Finally, on 7 November 1805, they reached the Pacific Ocean. The trip was approximately two thousand miles long. The explorers began their trip back to Saint Louis in March 1806 and returned home the following September.

Objective

To determine which of two line graphs represents a given story and to justify the choice

Directions

1. Separate students into groups of three to five. Give each student a copy of the "Lewis and Clark and Me" activity sheet.

2. Direct students to look at the three graphs at the top of the activity sheet. Have the groups compare and contrast the appearance of the graphs and discuss their findings.

3. Ask students to read the story of the imaginary trip printed underneath the graphs. Direct each group to determine which graph depicts the story and to complete the sentence at the end of the story.

Prepared by Martha H. (Marty) Hopkins *and* Diane M. Gard
Edited by Daniel J. Brahier *and* William R. Speer

4. Have each group share its decisions. Encourage groups to discuss how and why they reached the conclusions they did.

5. Direct the students to look at the graph of Lewis and Clark's expedition. Have the students read and discuss the background information printed beside the graph.

6. Ask the following questions and then discuss the students' responses as a class: How many months did Lewis and Clark take to reach the Pacific Ocean? About how many days is eighteen months? About how many months did they take to make the return trip?

7. Instruct students to use the graph as a guide to write a story that details what may have happened on the expedition. Have students share and discuss their stories.

Answers

Graph B best represents the imaginary trip. Graph A covers only 25 miles per hour for two hours on the interstate, which is possible, especially with congestion, but then this graph shows that you are stopped for the three hours you were sightseeing on the country road. During the time you stopped for lunch, this graph shows you traveling 75 miles. During your two additional hours of country-road driving, this graph depicts you somehow losing total miles traveled. The remainder of graph A is consistent with the story after the eighth hour.

Graph C covers 200 miles in two hours on the interstate, which is possible but rather fast and definitely illegal. For the three hours on country roads, the graph shows that you travel 800 miles, averaging more than 265 MPH. When you stop for lunch, graph C shows that you suddenly lose all the mileage you have traveled, and after lunch you cover 100 miles on country roads, for a fairly speedy average of 50 MPH. In the two hours on the interstate that follow, graph C represents 700 miles traveled, for a much-too-fast average of 350 MPH.

Applicable Standards

- **Communication**
- **Reasoning**
- **Connections**
- **Statistics**

Students' stories about the Lewis and Clark graph should allow for the winter stop represented by the horizontal line from the fifth month to the eleventh month. The story should also note that Lewis and Clark were slowed by the mountains and other hostile situations before they increased the speed of their trip as they approached the Pacific Ocean.

Extensions

1. Instruct the students to write a story about a trip to explore their state. Remind them that their stories must accurately account for the relation of time and distance depicted in one of the graphs on the activity sheet.

2. Have teams of students write a brief story about a trip from home to school. On a separate sheet, have them draw a line graph that represents their story. Put all the stories in a basket and tape all the graphs to the chalkboard. Then have each team select a story and locate the corresponding graph. This activity could also be conducted in reverse. As an aid in creating the graphs, suggest that students draw time on the horizontal axis and distance on the vertical axis. Then discuss reversing these axes and the effect of this reversal on the appearance of the graph.

Family Activity

See "Exploring Speed" on page 120.

Name _____

Lewis and Clark and Me

Graphs can sometimes be used to show how time and distance are related. The three graphs below are supposed to represent the same trip. Pretend that you took the trip described in the story below. Read the story of your trip and determine which of the graphs best represents your journey.

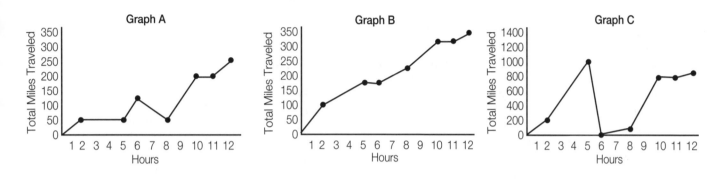

You left your home at 8 A.M. and drove along the interstate for two hours. At about 10 A.M., you decided to get off the interstate highway and travel on a bumpy and curvy country road so you could sightsee. For the next three hours, you took your time and enjoyed the view. At 1 P.M., you got hungry, so you stopped and had some lunch. You got back on the road about 2 P.M. and continued along country roads for two more hours. At 4 P.M., you got back on the interstate and stayed on it for the next two hours. Unfortunately, just as you were about to get off the interstate, you got a flat tire. After changing your tire, you drove to your friend's house, where you spent the night.

I think this story is illustrated by graph _____ because _____

_____

_____

Use the background information and the graph below to write a story about what you think happened on Lewis and Clark's expedition. Use your imagination, but remember that your story must be reasonable. Be sure to consider such factors as seasons and weather, type of route (land or water), encounters with Native Americans, illness, and so on, that would have affected Lewis and Clark's travel.

Background information: Lewis and Clark set out on 14 May 1804 to explore the northwestern part of the Louisiana Purchase. They left from Saint Louis, Missouri, and traveled northwest until they finally reached the Pacific Ocean.

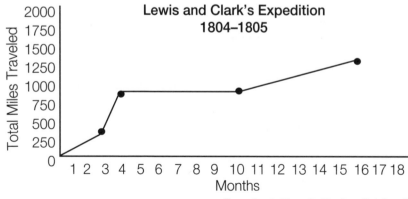

From the *Arithmetic Teacher*, October 1992

IDEAS

Space Nutrition

LEVELS 6–8

Background

NASA has found that astronauts must maintain a daily nutritional level to perform to their potential while on a space-shuttle mission. In this activity, students use a calorie chart to determine serving sizes that will ensure that the astronauts are able to meet their work requirements. Each astronaut is given three individually packaged meals each day that ensure that they can consume at least 3000 calories during a twenty-four-hour period. Meals are similar to those served on Earth except that some of the ingredients may be freeze-dried or irradiated. The caloric content for an individual food item is the same regardless of the manner in which the food is packaged for the mission.

Information about each space mission, the effects of space flight on humans, the importance of research developments to our lives on Earth, the exploration of planets, astronauts, and so on, is available to teachers by contacting the National Aeronautics and Space Administration, Education and Awareness Branch, John F. Kennedy Space Center, Kennedy Space Center, FL 32899.

Objective

To use computation and estimation techniques to explore relationships among various number combinations that yield a given total

Directions

1. Discuss the importance of proper nutrition, even when working in weightless conditions. Encourage discussion about calorie intake and its role in supplying energy.

2. Reproduce a copy of the "Space Nutrition" activity sheet for each student. Since it is important that students have an opportunity to explain their thinking and the reasoning behind the decisions they make, allow students to complete the activity sheet in pairs or in a small group of three or four students.

3. Introduce the activity sheet, discussing appropriate serving sizes. Point out that an astronaut must eat every item on the menu but that serving sizes of the items can be varied.

4. In their small groups, students should make choices regarding appropriate serving sizes and determine the overall caloric content of the meals. They may need to be reminded of the condition that the *daily* caloric content must be between 3000 and 4000 calories.

5. On completion of the activity sheet, encourage groups to compare the serving sizes they chose. It is important that they realize that many correct answers are possible. As each group presents its solution to the problem, discuss the problem-solving process used by the group as well as the appropriateness of the serving sizes chosen.

Answers

Answers will vary from group to group. Each group should be certain to include each menu item in the day's diet. Total calories must be within the 3000 to 4000 range.

Prepared by Martha H. (Marty) Hopkins *and* Diane M. Gard
Edited by Daniel J. Brahier *and* William R. Speer

Applicable Standards

- **Connections**
- **Computation and Estimation**

Extensions

1. Challenge the students to plan a week of meals meeting the criteria stated in the background section of this activity. Note that the activity sheet already includes data on various other food items that can be used. Encourage students to collect data regarding serving sizes and the caloric content of foods not on the chart as necessary to ensure that the astronauts enjoy a different menu every day.

2. Have the students research the nutritional requirements for a typical junior high school or middle school student. Compare the suggested caloric requirements of a student with those of an astronaut. Discuss the differences in the diets as well. What foods are not available to the astronauts (e.g., milk)? Why do you think these foods are restricted?

3. This activity lends itself well to the use of a simple spreadsheet program on a computer. By taking full advantage of the power of a spreadsheet, students are more readily encouraged to make conjectures and to test the impact of these conjectures.

Family activity

See "Exploring Speed" on page 120.

Space Nutrition

Name _____

Congratulations! You have just been hired to plan meals for astronauts flying on the space shuttle! NASA has determined the following nutrition requirements for this mission: (1) Each astronaut must eat three meals a day; (2) each astronaut needs to take in at least 3000 calories each day to complete all tasks on board the spacecraft; (3) each astronaut is limited to no more than 4000 calories a day; and (4) each astronaut must have a portion of every item listed on the menu below. As an apprentice nutrition specialist, your first job is to determine the most appropriate serving sizes for each meal. Good luck!

Approximate Caloric Content of Some Common Foods

Beverages (calories per ounce)
Apple juice 14
Cocoa (in 1 cup water) 102
Grape drink 20
Lemonade. 13
Orange drink 14

Breads (calories per piece)
Sweet roll 112
Pancakes 164
White bread 76
Whole-wheat bread 67
Chocolate-chip cookie. 50

Miscellaneous (calories)
Jam . . . . 54 per Tbsp.
Mayonnaise . . . . 51 per Tbsp.
Peanut butter . . . . 94 per Tbsp.
Butter or margarine . . . . . 36 per pat
Honey . . . . 64 per Tbsp.
Syrup . . . . 60 per Tbsp.
Cheese. . . . . 70 per 1-in. cube
Shrimp cocktail in sauce 150
Scrambled eggs (1 egg) 110

Fruits (calories per piece)
Apples. 80
Bananas 101
Blueberries (one-half cup) 45
Grapes 4
Peaches 58
Raisins (one-third cup) 124

Meats (calories per ounce)
Beef 73
Bacon (per slice) 43
Bologna 85
Ham 68
Sausage (2 oz.) 125

Vegetables (calories per cup)
Broccoli. 40
Carrots 48
Corn 140
Peas 122
Potatoes (per potato) 145
Tomatoes (per tomato) 40

Other (calories per cup)
Chicken à la king 468
Macaroni and cheese 430
Spaghetti and meatballs 332
Chocolate pudding 386
Cream of mushroom soup 120

Food item	Serving size	Number of calories
Breakfast		
Orange drink		
Peaches		
Scrambled eggs		
Sausage		
Cocoa		
Sweet roll		
Lunch		
Cream of mushroom soup		
Ham-and-cheese sandwich		
Stewed tomatoes		
Banana		
Cookies		
Grape drink		
Dinner		
Shrimp cocktail		
Beefsteak		
Broccoli au gratin		
Grapes		
Chocolate pudding		
Cocoa		

Breakfast total: _____

Lunch total: _____

Dinner total: _____

Grand total: _____

Sources: *Rodale's Basic Natural Foods Cookbook*, Charles Gerras, ed. (New York: Fireside Paperbacks, 1989) and *Joy of Cooking*, Irma S. Rombauer and Marion R. Becker (Greenwich, Conn.: Macmillan, 1985)

From the *Arithmetic Teacher*, October 1992

Which Way?

LEVELS 5–6

Background

During the first few weeks of school, students often explore various ways of getting to and from school. This activity encourages students' solving problems in which they compare, contrast, and apply map-reading and map-interpretation skills.

Objective

To identify and use appropriate problem-solving strategies involving patterning and incorporating informal coordinate geometry

Directions

1. Make and distribute a copy of the "Which Way?" activity sheet for each student. Teachers might want to allow for small-group work during this activity to encourage discussion and sharing of ideas.

2. Discuss with the students the nature of the problem in questions 1, 2, and 3, pointing out that sometimes many ways can be used to solve a problem and that many factors must be taken into account.

3. Note that questions 4 and 5 remove the restriction of traveling only east and south but add the requirement that three specific points must be connected.

4. Question 6 adds the element of time delays to the decision-making process. Encourage students to explore several different methods of solution to this problem.

Prepared by Daniel J. Brahier, Shirley Hodapp, Rebecca Martin, *and* William R. Speer
Edited by William R. Speer

Answers

1. Six blocks long

2. Twenty different routes are possible by traveling only east and south.

3. If the student followed directions for direct routes, then any direct route is an example of a shortest possible route. All direct routes are six blocks long. A total of three blocks south and three blocks east must be traveled regardless of the order in which they are traveled.

4. Answers will vary.

5. The shortest possible route for the bus, given the bus stops shown, is fourteen blocks (8 blocks to the student's house and 6 blocks back to the school). This number is obtained by going through stop B first, then stop A. If the bus goes through stop A first, then the minimum distance is sixteen blocks (10 blocks to the student's house and 6 blocks back to the school).

6. The quickest route would take thirteen minutes and is shown on the grid in figure 1. The numbers in the circles indicate the time in minutes necessary to get from that corner to the park. The arrows on the circles show the direc-

tion to go to get to the park in that amount of time.

Extensions

1. Ask the students to imagine that they live in Anytown, Ohio, and that they are the director of transportation for the Anytown School District. The district owns five buses. What other information would the transportation director need to determine which routes the buses should follow?

2. If the transportation director wanted the buses to cover about the same area, how would he or she divide the town into routes? If each of the buses is to carry about the same number of students, would the routes be divided any differently?

Family activity

See "Shopping Spree" on page 122.

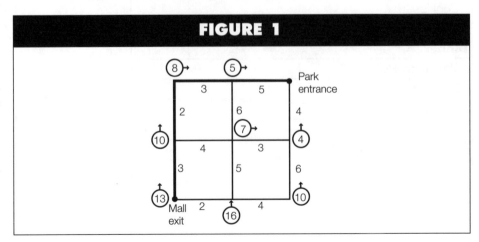

FIGURE 1

Name _____

Which Way?

Your house is at the corner of Elm and First Streets. The school is at Fourth and Oak Streets. On the first day of school, you decide to walk to school, but you want to find a direct route. Because of houses, fences, and other obstacles, you must walk only along the streets. On a direct route from your home to school, you will always travel east or south, never west or north.

1. Trace a direct route on the map from your house to school. How many blocks long is your route?_____

2. How many different direct routes could you take from your house to school? _____

3. Was the direct route that you traced the shortest possible route from your house to school?_____ Can more than one route be the shortest?_____ Explain your answer. _____

_____

_____

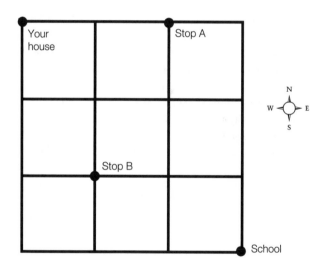

On the second day of school you decide to take the bus rather than walk. The grid shows the locations of bus stops between your house and the school. Luckily, the last stop the bus makes before heading back to school is right in front of your house!

4. Trace any path from the school through all the bus stops and back to school (here buses can travel north, south, east, or west).

5. How many blocks did the bus travel over the route that you traced in question 4?_____ Is this route the shortest possible one for the bus? _____ Explain.

_____

_____

On the weekend, you decide to go shopping and to a ball game. The numbers on the grid represent the time in minutes required to travel over the indicated part of the route. Because of construction, traffic lights, special speed zones, and other factors, some routes of equal distance have very different travel times.

6. Find the quickest route from the mall exit to the park entrance. Trace your solution route, and be prepared to explain your strategy to a classmate.

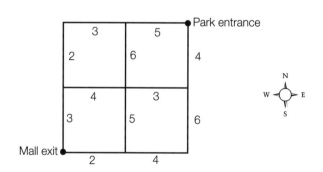

From the *Arithmetic Teacher*, September 1992

Lock It Up

LEVELS 7–8

Background

Students entering into a different kind of school setting become aware of the experience of using lockers. Problem solving and probability are parts of this experience.

Objective

To use data analysis and probability as a means of solving problems

Directions

1. Reproduce a "Lock It Up" activity sheet for each student.

2. Discuss with students the need for, and uses of, lockers in junior high or middle school. Record all locker numbers represented in the class. Discuss the probability of each student's being assigned the specific locker number he or she actually received. Focus on the possible rationale for the system used to assign lockers to all students in the building. Factors that might influence decisions include the number and placement of homerooms, lockers, and bus stops.

3. Divide students into small groups and give each group a "Lock It Up" activity sheet. Have the groups solve the problems posed.

4. Facilitate small-group work as needed.

Answers

1. Five 0's, fifteen 1's, fifteen 2's, fifteen 3's, fifteen 4's, six 5's, five 6's, five 7's, five 8's, and five 9's are required to number all the lockers.

2. The probability that a locker number contains an "8" is 0.1 (5 out of 50). The probability that a locker number contains an "8" or a "2" is 0.36 (18 out of 50).

3. The number of students other than you who might have locks having the same three numbers in the combination is five ($3 \times 2 \times 1 - 1$), namely, 3-32-17, 17-3-32, 17-32-3, 32-17-3, and 32-3-17. The number of locks having combinations using nonconsecutive repetition of these numbers is six ($3 \times 2 \times 1$), namely, 3-17-3, 3-32-3, 17-32-17, 32-17-32, 17-3-17, and 32-3-32.

Applicable Standards

- **Problem Solving**
- **Probability**

Extension

Imagine that you are given the opportunity to design a totally different kind of lock for the lockers. You may use neither numbers nor keys. As a group, decide how you might design a lock and what you would use to open it. *Teacher's note:* If the students have a problem focusing on this task, suggest some of the following: a bar-code system, a credit-card ID system, a token system, or a voice-activation system. The students need to think about how people gain access to other secured systems in the real world, such as gasoline pumps, hotel rooms, and safe deposit boxes.

Family activity

See "Shopping Spree" on page 122.

Prepared by Daniel J. Brahier, Shirley Hodapp, Rebecca Martin, *and* William R. Speer

Edited by William R. Speer

Name _____

Lock It Up

1. The fifty lockers in the hall at school have been painted over the summer break in the two school colors. The custodian has been assigned the task of replacing the numbers on the lockers. The lockers will be numbered consecutively from 1 to 50. Help the custodian figure how many of each digit are needed to complete the task of numbering the lockers from 1 to 50.

   0 _____ 1 _____ 2 _____ 3 _____ 4 _____

   5 _____ 6 _____ 7 _____ 8 _____ 9 _____

   Explain how you went about solving this problem. Describe your method in words so that another student can use your approach. _____

   _____

   Find someone in class who has a different way to arrive at the solution.

2. The warehouse calls to say that the digit "8" is temporarily out of stock. What is the probability of being assigned a locker having this missing digit? _____ The warehouse also discovers that they are out of the digit "2." What is the probability that your locker is missing at least one of these two digits?_____

3. You are assigned locker number 46, and your locker combination is 3-17-32. This combination is just one of many using these three numbers. How many other students might have locks that have combinations having these same three numbers but in a different order? _____ How many locks could have combinations using some or all of these three numbers but only these three numbers if the numbers are repeated but not consecutively (e.g., a combination could be 3-17-3 but not 3-3-17)? _____ Explain how you arrived at your answers. _____

   _____

   _____

From the *Arithmetic Teacher*, September 1992

Computation Court: Verify the Verdict

LEVELS 4-6

Objectives

Case 1: To solve multistep problems using mental-mathematics techniques

Case 2: To solve real-world problems involving the multiplication of decimals

Case 3: To solve real-world problems involving the addition and subtraction of fractions

Directions

1. Discuss the role of a judge in deciding a court case, emphasizing the need to justify the decision. Tell students that in "computation court," problem solutions are judged correct or incorrect.

2. Reproduce a copy of the activity sheet for each student.

3. Study each case separately. Read aloud each problem and its solution. Encourage students to decide the verdict individually.

4. After students have made a decision, ask them to write the reason for their decision.

5. Because students' reasoning may vary greatly, encourage them to share their answers with other members of the class.

Important questions

1. Are the answers reasonable?

2. For incorrect solutions, where did the solution process break down?

3. How do you know when the problem is solved?

4. In case 1, why does the process work?

Extensions

1. Discuss and demonstrate other solution strategies that could be used for each problem.

2. Prepare correct or incorrect solutions to problems found in the students' textbooks for them to analyze and discuss.

Applicable Standards

- **Reasoning**
- **Computation and Estimation**

3. After discussing why the solution in case 1 is correct, have students practice this strategy with such other numbers as 31×99 and 42×97.

Answers

Case 1: Juanita's solution is correct.

Case 2: Sam's solution is incorrect.

Case 3: Pedro's solution is incorrect.

Family activity

See "Computation Court: Home-Court Advantage" on page 124.

Prepared by Martha H. (Marty) Hopkins
Edited by Francis (Skip) Fennell

Computation Court: Verify the Verdict

Case 1

Juanita wanted to buy 15 party favors that cost 98 cents each and 15 that cost 95 cents each. She didn't have her calculator with her. This is how she figured out how much the party favors would cost:

> If each of the favors costs $1.00, it would be $30.00. But 15 of them cost $0.02 less than $1.00, so that's $0.30 less. The others cost $0.05 less than $1.00, so that would be another $0.75 less. The total bill should be $30.00 – 0.30 – 0.75, or $28.95.

Verdict: ☐ Juanita's solution is correct.   ☐ Juanita's solution is incorrect.

Explain how you know. _____

_____

Case 2

Sam's class is making chili for the school fair. The class decided that they will need 13 pounds of ground beef. Sam priced the beef at $2.47 a pound. He figured the cost of the beef like this:

> We need 13 pounds of beef and each pound costs $2.47, so I must multiply 13 × $2.47.
>
> $$\begin{array}{r} 2.47 \\ \times\ \ 13 \\ \hline 741 \\ 247\ \ \\ \hline \$9.88 \end{array}$$
>
> The beef will cost us $9.88.

Verdict: ☐ Sam's solution is correct.   ☐ Sam's solution is incorrect.
Explain how you know. _____

_____

Case 3

Henry and Sal ordered a pizza. Henry ate 1/4 of it, and Sal ate 1/2 of it. They took the rest to their friend Pedro. Pedro wanted to find out how generous his friends were. This is how he figured:

> Henry ate 1/4 of the pizza, and Sal ate 1/2. Since 1/4 + 1/2 = 2/8, together they ate 2/8 of the pizza. Since 8/8 – 2/8 = 6/8, I get to eat 6/8, or 3/4, of the pizza.

Verdict: ☐ Pedro's solution is correct.   ☐ Pedro's solution is incorrect.
Explain how you know. _____

_____

From the *Arithmetic Teacher*, May 1992

IDEAS

Computation Court: Defend Your Decision

LEVELS 6–8

Objectives

Case 1: To solve a real-world problem involving the multiplication of fractions

Case 2: To solve problems involving double-digit multiplication using mental-mathematics techniques

Case 3: (*a*) To solve real-world problems involving the division of decimals; (*b*) to recognize the meaning of the remainder in the context of a real-world problem

Directions

1. Discuss the role of a judge in deciding a court case, emphasizing the need to justify the decision. Tell students that in "computation court," the problem solution is judged correct or incorrect.

2. Reproduce a copy of the activity sheet for each student.

3. Study each case separately. Read aloud the problem and the solutions. Encourage students to decide the verdict individually. Remind the students that for problems for which more than one solution is given, both solutions may be correct. After the students have made a decision, ask them to write the reason for their decision.

4. Because students' reasoning may vary greatly, encourage them to share their answers with other members of the class.

Important questions

1. Are the answers reasonable?

2. For incorrect solutions, where did the solution process break down?

3. How do you know when the problem is solved?

4. In case 2, why do the solution processes work?

Extensions

1. Discuss and demonstrate other solution strategies that could be used for each problem.

2. Prepare correct or incorrect solutions to problems found in the students' textbooks for them to analyze and discuss.

3. After discussing why the solutions in case 2 are correct, have students practice these strategies with such other numbers as 15×3.26 and 15×14.98.

4. When analyzing Indira's and Maureen's solutions, discuss the role of estimation in computation and the variety of strategies that can be used.

Answers

Case 1: David's solution is correct.

Case 2: Both solutions are reasonable.

Case 3: Maureen's solution is correct.

Family activity

See "Computation Court: Home-Court Advantage" on page 124.

Prepared by Martha H. (Marty) Hopkins
Edited by Francis (Skip) Fennell

Computation Court: Defend Your Decision

Case 1

A muffin recipe calls for 1/2 cup of sugar. Sarah and David want to make 3/4 of a recipe. They decide in these ways how much sugar to use:

I must divide 1/2 cup by 3/4, so

$$\frac{1}{2} \div \frac{3}{4} = \frac{1}{2} \times \frac{4}{3} = \frac{4}{6} = \frac{2}{3}.$$

I must use 2/3 cup of sugar.

I must multiply 1/2 cup by 3/4,

$$\frac{1}{2} \times \frac{3}{4} = \frac{3}{8}.$$

I must use 3/8 cup of sugar.

Verdict: ☐ Sarah's solution is correct. ☐ David's solution is correct. ☐ Neither solution is correct.
Explain how you know. _____
_____

Case 2

Julio and Indira want to buy 15 cans of fruit that cost $0.62 each. They aren't sure they have enough money, and neither of them has a calculator. This is how each figures out how much the fruit costs:

10 × 62 = 620; half as much as that is 310; 620 + 310 = 930. The fruit costs $9.30.

Each can costs a little bit more than $0.60. We need 15 cans. 15 × 60 = 900, so the fruit costs a little more than $9.00.

Verdict: ☐ Julio's solution is correct. ☐ Indira's solution is correct. ☐ Both solutions are reasonable.
Explain how you know. _____
_____

Case 3

Malik and Maureen want to take some friends to an amusement park to celebrate their birthday. Admission to the park is $15.75 per person. They can spend no more than $100.00. This is how each figures out how many friends they can invite:

I must divide $100.00 by $15.75.

```
          6.3
15.75 ) 100.000
        9450
        5500
        4725
         775
```

The answer is 6.3, but we can't take 0.3 of a friend, so we can invite 6 friends to go with us to the amusement park.

Each person costs a little more than $15. Six 15s are in 100, so about 6 people can go. There are 2 of us, so we can invite 4 friends to the amusement park.

Verdict: ☐ Malik's solution is correct. ☐ Maureen's solution is correct. ☐ Neither solution is correct.
Explain how you know. _____
_____

IDEAS

The World's Fastest

LEVELS 4–8

Background

In this activity, students will work with time and linear measurement. Students will measure 100 meters and actually run 100 meters, timing one another using a stopwatch. They will also interpret data from a table.

Objective

To estimate the length of 100 meters, estimate time in seconds, and interpret data

Directions

1. Tell the students to raise their hands after they think ten seconds has passed. Ask the students what strategies they used to determine ten seconds. Ask them to raise their hands after thirty seconds. Was it easier to determine ten or thirty seconds? Why?

2. Ask the students to think about a distance of 100 meters. Have the students name some distances that are about 100 meters long (e.g., longer than a football field, about the length of three moving vans or school buses).

3. Ask the students how long they think it would take someone to run 100 meters.

4. Distribute the activity sheet "The World's Fastest." Have the students look at the chart of data and draw some conclusions about the records for the 100-meter dash. Guide the students to compare the times for the men and women.

5. Have the students complete questions 1–6. Discuss the answers after they have finished.

Prepared by Kay B. Sammons *and* Beth Kobett
Edited by Francis (Skip) Fennell

6. Take the students out to a field and have them measure 100 meters and set up start and finish lines.

7. Have students use a stopwatch to time one another in the 100-meter dash. Have students run twice and record their times. The trials can be done on the same day or on subsequent days. Have them record their personal-best time in question 7.

8. Return to the classroom and have students record their time on their activity sheet and on a class chart like the one shown. Then complete questions 8 and 9.

Students' names	Personal best

Extensions

1. Record all class times on a line plot similar to that shown. Record boys' and girls' times in different colors. Elementary school students are likely to have a range of times from sixteen seconds to thirty seconds.

```
      X  X
      X  X        XXX
   ◄──┼────┼────┼────┼────┼──►
     15   20   25   30   35
```

Ask the following questions:

a) Is this sample typical for students your age?

b) Would the times for younger students be generally faster or slower?

How could we find out?

c) Would the teachers on our staff generally run faster or slower?

2. Examine the historical background of the Olympic Games. Have the students determine why the Olympics were not held in some years. (During World Wars I and II the Olympics were not held.) Ask the students to locate the countries where the Olympics have been held.

Answers

1. A little less than one second, or a little more than a half second

2. 1988

3. The women's times improved except for 1972 and 1980. The men's times improved except for 1952, 1972, and 1980.

4–7. Answers will vary.

8. Answers will vary. For the men's dash, answers between 9.6 and 10.5 seconds would be reasonable. The actual winning time was 9.96 seconds. For the women's dash, answers between 10.25 and 11.5 seconds would be reasonable. The actual winning time was 10.82.

9. Better physical fitness, better conditions for running, good running shoes, and so on

Name _____

The World's Fastest

Year	Women's Champion	Country	Time (seconds)	Men's Champion	Country	Time (seconds)
1928	Elizabeth Robinson	U.S.	12.2	Percy Williams	Can.	10.8
1936	Helen Stephens	U.S.	11.5	Jesse Owens	U.S.	10.3
1952	Marjorie Jackson	Australia	11.5	Lindy Remigino	U.S.	10.4
1960	Wilma Rudolph	U.S.	11.0	Armin Hary	W. Ger.	10.2
1968	Wyomia Tyus	U.S.	11.00	Jim Hines	U.S.	9.95
1972	Renate Stecher	E. Ger.	11.07	Valery Borzov	USSR	10.14
1980	Lyudmila Kondratyeva	USSR	11.60	Allan Wells	G.B.	10.25
1988	Florence Griffith-Joyner	U.S.	10.54	Carl Lewis	U.S.	9.92

Source: *The World Almanac and Book of Facts*, edited by Mark S. Hoffman {New York: Pharos Books, 1991}

The chart includes some of the male and female Olympic winners of the 100-meter dash. Refer to the information in the table to answer the questions.

1. About how much faster did Carl Lewis run than Florence Griffith-Joyner? _____

2. In what year did the women's time come closest to the men's time? _____

3. Describe how the winning time improved for men and women from 1928 to 1988.

   _____

   _____

4. List three things that you can do in about 9 seconds. _____

   _____

5. Name three distances that are about 100 meters long. _____

   _____

6. Predict how fast you can run 100 meters. _____ Try it!

7. My time was _____. Describe your time in relation to any of the Olympic times above.

   Is it twice as long? _____ Three times as long? _____

8. Consider the 1992 Olympics. What do you think might have been the winning time for men? _____

   For women? _____

9. What factors might explain the improvements in the record over time? Explain your answer. _____

   _____

From the *Arithmetic Teacher*, April 1992

Weight Toss

Background

The students will estimate and measure length and organize and interpret data. They will throw a softball, measure the distance of the throw, record the class's measurements, and analyze the class's data.

Objective

To estimate and measure lengths involving fractions and to organize and interpret data

Directions

1. Distribute a "Weight Toss" activity sheet to each student and ask the students to review and describe the Olympics data.

2. Discuss objects that are about 75 feet long. Elicit from the students what benchmarks they used to decide which objects have lengths of about 75 feet.

3. The men's shot weighs 16 pounds. Elicit from the students other items that weigh about 16 pounds. If possible, find something that weighs 16 pounds and ask the students to hold it. Ask the students how many mathematics books would have a total weight of about 16 pounds.

4. Tell the students that instead of throwing a 16-pound shot, they will be throwing a softball overhand and underhand. Have the students complete the following:

a) Estimate how far you can throw a softball overhand.

b) Record in feet on a line plot (see example) the estimates for an overhand throw in one color and an underhand throw in a second color.

```
                          X
   X   X                  X
 ──┼──┼──┼──┼──┼──┼──┼──┼──┼──┼──►
  20 30 40 50 60 70 80 90 100 110 120
```

c) On a playing field, draw a chalk circle with a diameter of 7 feet. This circle is the same size as the shot-put circle at the Olympic Games. Next, have the students measure benchmarks in units of 10 feet. Each student should throw the softball once underhand and once overhand then record the throws in feet and inches on another line plot, using different colors for underhand and overhand throws.

d) Have the students estimate the degrees at which they throw the ball in relation to the ground for both the underhand and overhand throws.

e) Discuss what effect the angle of the throws might have on the length of the throws.

f) Have the students use a calculator to determine the class's average lengths of underhand and overhand throws.

Extensions

Have the students compare the women's Olympics distances for the shot put (see table 1). The weight of the women's shot is 8 pounds, 13 ounces. Using this information, have the students compare the lengths of men's and women's throws. Lead the students to recognize that the winning distances for men and women have become closer in recent years. In 1980, the women's distance was greater than the men's distance. In 1984, both the men's and women's records were less than in 1980. Have the students discuss possible reasons for this occurrence.

1. Starting in 1948, compare the winning distances for men and women. What trends do students notice?

2. What factors might influence the winning toss for each Olympics?

Answers

1, 4–5, 7–9. Answers will vary.

2. About 37 feet, or about twice as far

3. The distance improved each year except for 1920 and 1984, when the distance was shorter than in the previous year.

6. About 1 pound

10. Answers will vary. Overhand will probably be longer.

11. Yes. As the angle of the throw approaches 45 degrees, the length of the throw increases if the force is the same.

Prepared by Kay B. Sammons *and* Beth Kobett
Edited by Francis (Skip) Fennell

Applicable Standards

- **Connections**
- **Computation and Estimation**
- **Measurement**

TABLE 1

Women's Shot Put

Year	Winner	Country	Distance		
1948	Micheline Ostermeyer	France	45 ft.	1	1/2 in.
1952	Galina Zybina	USSR	50 ft.	1	3/4 in.
1956	Tamara Tishkyevich	USSR	54 ft.	5	in.
1960	Tamara Press	USSR	56 ft.	10 in.	
1964	Tamara Press	USSR	59 ft.	6	1/4 in.
1968	Margitta Gummel	E. Ger.	64 ft.	4 in.	
1972	Nadezhda Chizova	USSR	69 ft.		
1976	Ivanka Hristova	Bulgaria	69 ft.	5	1/4 in.
1980	Ilona Slupianek	E. Ger.	73 ft.	6	1/4 in.
1984	Claudia Losch	W. Ger.	67 ft.	2	1/4 in.
1988	Natalya Lisovskaya	USSR	72 ft.	11 1/2 in.	

Source: *The World Almanac and Book of Facts*, edited by Mark S. Hoffman (New York: Pharos Books, 1991)

Name _____

Weight Toss

The chart below gives information about Olympics shot-put winners and their tosses.

Year	Winner	Country	Distance
1896	Robert Garrett	U.S.	36 ft. 9 3/4 in.
1900	Richard Sheldon	U.S.	46 ft. 3 1/4 in.
1912	Pat McDonald	U.S.	50 ft. 4 in.
1920	Ville Porhola	Finland	48 ft. 7 1/4 in.
1928	John Kuck	U.S.	52 ft. 3/4 in.
1936	Hans Woellke	Ger.	53 ft. 1 3/4 in.
1948	Wilbur Thompson	U.S.	56 ft. 2 in.
1956	Parry O'Brien	U.S.	60 ft. 11 1/4 in.
1960	William Nieder	U.S.	64 ft. 6 3/4 in.
1964	Dallas Long	U.S.	66 ft. 8 1/2 in.
1968	Randy Matson	U.S.	67 ft. 4 3/4 in.
1976	Udo Beyer	E. Ger.	69 ft. 3/4 in.
1980	Vladimir Kiselyov	USSR	70 ft. 1/2 in.
1984	Alessandro Andrei	Italy	69 ft. 9 in.
1988	Ulf Timmermann	E. Ger.	73 ft. 8 3/4 in.

Source: *The World Almanac and Book of Facts,* edited by Mark S. Hoffman (New York: Pharos Books, 1991)

1. The winning shot put in the 1988 Olympics was 73 feet 8 3/4 inches long. Name three things that are about 75 feet in length.

   _____

   _____

2. About how much farther did Ulf Timmermann put the shot than Robert Garrett?

   _____

3. How did the winning Olympics shot-put distance change from 1896 to 1988?

   _____

   _____

4. The shot weighs 16 pounds. Name two things that weigh about 16 pounds.

   _____

   _____

5. Imagine throwing 16 pounds. About how far do you think you could toss such a weight? _____

6. About how much does a softball weigh? _____

   Describe the weight of the softball in relation to that of the shot. _____

   Could you throw a softball about the same distance, a shorter distance, or a longer distance than you could throw a shot? _____

7. About how far do you think you could throw a softball? _____ Estimate in feet the length of an overhand and underhand throw.   Overhand _____   Underhand _____

8. The shot is thrown at about a 40-degree angle. As you throw the softball, estimate the angle of the underhand and overhand throws.   Overhand _____   Underhand _____

9. Throw a softball twice, once overhand and once underhand. Measure the length of each throw and record it on the class chart and here.   Overhand _____   Underhand _____

   Which throw was longer? _____

10. Using a calculator, determine a class average for the underhand throw and the overhand throw. In your class, which throw was longer on average? _____

11. Does the degree at which a softball is thrown affect the length of the throw? _____

    Explain. _____

From the *Arithmetic Teacher,* April 1992

Fraction Kites in Motion

LEVELS 5–6

Objective

Given the numerator of one fraction and the denominator of the other, the students create pairs of fractions that have sums or differences close to 1/2, 1, and 2.

Materials

A copy of the "Fraction Kites in Motion" activity sheet for each student

Directions

1. Discuss with students how to determine if a fraction is closer to 0, 1/2, or 1. Ask the students what strategies they would use to determine where a fraction falls on a number line from 0 to 1. How do you know where to put 5/6, 13/16, or 1/8? Have the students demonstrate on an overhead projector where to place the fractions on a number line like the one shown:

0   1

2. Give the students two fractions with the numerator missing from one and the denominator missing from the other, for instance, 3/? and ?/4. Ask the students, "If I want to add these two fractions to make a fraction very close to 1, what numbers should I put in the numerator and denominator? Is more than one answer possible?"

3. Distribute the activity sheet to each student or to pairs of students. Have the students work independently or in pairs

4. Discuss with the students the questions at the bottom of the activity sheet.

Applicable Standards

- **Number and Number Relationships**
- **Computation and Estimation**

Extensions

1. Have the students use a calculator to verify their choices.

2. Change the numbers on the kites to 1 1/2, 2 1/2, and 3. Ask, "How does this change affect the fractions to be added?"

Prepared by Kay B. Sammons *and* Beth Kobett
Edited by Francis (Skip) Fennell

Name _____

Fraction Kites in Motion

Fill in the numerator or denominator so that the sum or difference is close to the amount indicated on the kite. Then answer the questions below. Do not use the some digit that is given in the portion of the fraction on the bow.

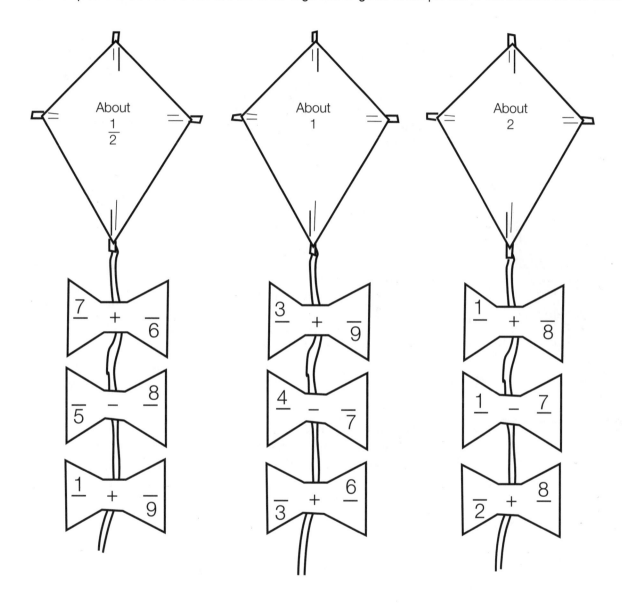

Talk about It

1. How did you decide what number to place in the numerator and denominator to make the sum or difference about 1/2, 1, or 2?

2. Which kite was the most difficult to complete? Why?

3. Which kite was the easiest to complete? Why?

From the *Arithmetic Teacher*, March 1992

High-Flying Fractions

LEVELS 6–8

Objective

The students estimate the sum, difference, or product of two fractions, two decimals, or one fraction and one decimal number.

Materials

1. One copy of the "High-Flying Fractions" activity sheet for each student

2. One set of index cards labeled with fractions and decimals as shown

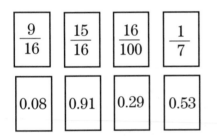

3. A chalkboard number line labeled 0 to 1, as shown

Directions

1. Draw a number line on the chalkboard and label it 0 to 1.

2. Distribute an index card to each student. Have the students work in pairs to determine where the fraction or decimal should be placed on the number line.

3. Have the students place the index cards on the number line and justify their placement. Ask questions like the following:

- Did you place your fraction closer to the 0 or the 1? Why?

- How did you decide where to place the fraction or decimal on the number line?

- Which were easier to place on the number line—the decimals or the fractions? Why?

- Which fractions and decimals were easier to place on the number line? Why?

- What strategy did you use to determine where to place the fractions and decimals?

Applicable Standard

- **Computation and Estimation**

4. Distribute a "High-Flying Fractions" activity sheet to each student. Have the students complete the activity and answer the questions.

5. Discuss the results with the students. Have the students determine all the combinations for each kite.

Extensions

1. Use the "High-Flying Fractions" activity sheet as a game board. Have the students take turns putting a fraction or decimal on each bow. The other student must then complete the bow to make the sum, difference, or product very close to 1/2, 1, or 2.

2. Use a calculator to verify estimates.

Prepared by Kay B. Sammons *and* Beth Kobett
Edited by Francis (Skip) Fennell

Name _____

High-Flying Fractions

Use the fractions and decimals below to make the value of each bow close to the number indicated on the kite. You may use the fractions and decimals more than once. Challenge: Use a combination of fractions and decimals in your problems!

$$\frac{1}{2} \quad \frac{9}{10} \quad \frac{9}{16} \quad \frac{12}{15} \quad \frac{5}{2} \quad \frac{7}{25} \quad \frac{8}{10} \quad \frac{9}{12} \quad \frac{15}{49} \quad \frac{22}{35} \quad \frac{18}{7} \quad \frac{9}{47}$$

0.65   0.21   0.33   0.45   1.6   0.79   0.94   0.39   0.089   3.03

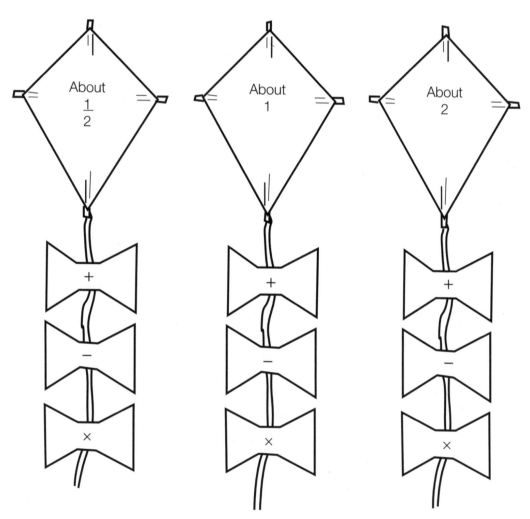

Talk about It

1. How did you decide what numbers to place on each bow to make the sum, difference, or product close to 1/2, 1, and 2?

2. Which kite was the most difficult to complete? Why?

3. Which kite was the easiest to complete? Why?

From the *Arithmetic Teacher*, March 1992

What's the Beat?

LEVELS 5–6

Background

In this activity, students use the average adult's number of heartbeats per minute to predict how many times the heart would beat during various lengths of time. The students also draw conclusions on the basis of information about the human heart rate and that of other animals.

Objective

To determine how many times the heart beats during various lengths of time, to use this information to compare numbers of heartbeats to units of time, and to draw conclusions about the heart rates of humans and animals

Directions

1. Reproduce a copy of the activity sheet for each student, and give each student or group of students a calculator.

2. Have the students read the introductory information, which gives the number of heartbeats per minute for the average adult at rest.

3. Have the students determine, using the average adult heart rate, the number of heartbeats for each length of time listed in 1*a–i*. Students should use a calculator and be prepared to discuss how they arrived at their answers. A range of answers is acceptable, even encouraged, depending on how the students solved the problems. The acceptable ranges are given in the answers

section. For example, some students may find the number of heartbeats in a day and then multiply by 28, 29, 30, or 31 to get the number of heartbeats in a month. Others may find the number of heartbeats in a week and multiply by 4 to obtain the number of heartbeats in a month. Some students may use 52 weeks, and others 365 days, in determining the number of heartbeats in a year. The ranges in the responses should be discussed. Note that calculators may overload when calculating the responses to 1*f–i*.

4. Using the answers in question 1, have the students complete questions 2–4 and discuss their responses.

5. Next have the students complete question 5. Discuss the students' responses and conclusions.

Answers

1. *a*) 4 200

   b) 100 800

   c) 705 600

   d) 2 822 400–3 124 800

   e) 36 288 000–36 892 800

   f) 362 880 000–368 928 000

   g) 725 760 000–737 856 000

   h) 1 088 640 000–1 106 784 000

   i) 2 358 720 000–2 398 032 000

2. In an hour the average heart beats 4 200 times, whereas an hour contains 3 600 seconds.

3. Yes, the average heart beats 70 times in a minute, whereas a minute contains 60 seconds.

4. About 10 days. By using the answer to 1*b*, if the heart beats about 100 000 times in one day, the heart would beat about 1 000 000 times in 10 days.

5. (*a*) Human's heartbeats per day: 100 800; shrew's heartbeats per day: 1 440 000; the shrew's heart beats 1 339 200 more times per day than the adult human's heart. (*b*) Human's heartbeats per day: 100 800; elephant's heartbeats per day: 43 200; the human's heart beats 57 600 more times per day than the elephant's. (*c*) The smaller the mammal, the greater is the number of heartbeats.

Extensions

1. Have groups of students choose various animals and predict each one's heart rate per minute. Have them graph the results of their predictions of the heart rates and the sizes of the animals.

2. Have the students determine in how many different ways they can find an acceptable response for the number-of-heartbeats activity (question 1).

Prepared by Lisa M. Passarello *and* Francis (Skip) Fennell

Name _____

What's the Beat?

When at rest, the normal adult heart beats about 70 times a minute.

1. How many times will the heart beat in—

    a) one hour? _____

    b) one day? _____

    c) one week? _____

    d) one month? _____

    e) one year? _____

    f) ten years? _____

    g) twenty years? _____

    h) thirty years? _____

    i) sixty-five years? _____

2. Which is the greater—the number of heartbeats in an hour or the number of seconds in an hour? _____

    How can you tell? _____

    _____

3. Does the heart best faster than once a second? _____

    How do you know? _____

    _____

4. What length of time is required for an average adult human's heart to beat 1 000 000 times? _____

    What helped you to make this decision? _____

5. When at rest, the blue whale's heart rate is 5 beats each minute, the elephant's is 30, and the adult human's is 70. The

    shrew, a mouselike animal, has a heart rate of about 1 000 beats a minute. _____

    a) About how many more times each day does the shrew's heart beat than the adult human's? _____

    b) About how many more times in one day does the adult human's heart beat than the elephant's? _____

    c) What conclusions can you draw from the information above? Write your response here. _____

    _____

    _____

From the *Arithmetic Teacher*, February 1992

IDEAS

Heartifacts

LEVELS 7–8

Background

This activity sheet deals with important facts about the heart. It involves students in interpreting factual information in a variety of problem-solving situations. Students also create and solve an original problem.

Objective

To interpret factual information, solve related problems, and create and solve an original problem

Directions

1. Reproduce a copy of the activity sheet for each student and give calculators to each student or group of students.

2. Have the students read and discuss the "fast facts" about the heart.

3. Tell the students to use the "fast facts" to solve problems 1–4 on the activity sheet. Discuss students' responses and how they arrived at their answers. Responses should fall in the range of answers given. For problem 2, discuss ways to use mental computation to determine one-half of 1 percent of a person's weight. Emphasize that the students should determine how they arrived at their estimate for problem 3.

4. Finally, have students use the "fast facts" to create an original problem of their own. They should solve the problem and then have a friend try to solve it.

Answers

1. Seventy beats a minute equals 100 800 times a day, or 36 288 000 times a year; 100 beats a minute equals 144 000 times a day, or 52 560 000 times a year. Both responses are based on a 365-day year.

2. Answers will vary according to students' weight.

3. About 7500 quarts each day. Estimate: The number of quarts pumped per hour is $5 \times 60 = 300$. 24 is close to 25 and $25 \times 3 = 75$, so $25 \times 300 = 7500$ quarts. Or, about 6500 to 7300 liters each day. Students might round the number of liters pumped per hour from 4.7 to 5 and the number of hours in a day to 25, so $5 \times 60 = 300$, and $300 \times 25 = 7500$. Since two numbers, 4.7 and 24, were rounded up, the 7500 estimate should be lowered, say, to 6500 to 7300.

4. After exercise, the heart would beat 112–122 times in one minute based on 70 beats a minute at rest or 160–175 times in one minute based on 100 beats a minute at rest.

5. Answers will vary.

Applicable Standards

- **Communication**
- **Computation and Estimation**

Extensions

1. Research other fast facts about the heart and design a fast-facts booklet with problems for the students to solve. Display the booklets in the classroom.

2. Have the students consult an aerobics or fitness instructor to determine a desirable target heart rate when exercising. Note that the maximum heart rate for one minute is estimated by subtracting a person's age from 220. The target heart rate for exercise is defined by the American Heart Association as 60–75 percent of the maximum heart rate. The target heart rate is high enough for conditioning but well within safe limits. Exercising at above 75 percent of the maximum heart rate is too strenuous for most people. Exercising at below 60 percent of the maximum heart rate gives the heart and lungs little conditioning. (Source: *Exercise and Your Heart* [American Heart Association 1990])

Prepared by Lisa M. Passarello *and* Francis (Skip) Fennell

Name _____

Heartifacts

Here are some "fast facts" about a most important machine—your heart:

- It weighs less than 1 pound, or about 0.5 kilogram.
- An adult's heart beats about 70 times a minute at rest.
- A child's heart beats about 100 times a minute at rest.
- The heart pumps 5 quarts, or 4.7 liters, of blood every minute.
- The heart does enough work in 1 hour to lift 1.4 metric tons more than 30 centimeters off the ground.

Using these facts, complete the following:

1. About how many times does your heart beat in a day? _____

   In a year? _____

2. The weight of the normal heart is about one-half of 1 percent of a person's total weight.

   How much do you think your heart weighs? _____

3. Estimate the amount of blood your heart pumps in one day. _____

   How did you determine your estimate? _____

4. After strenuous exercise, the heart can beat as much as 2.5 times faster than when at rest. It is more likely to beat between 1.6 and 1.75 times its resting rate. Let's say you ran a 10-kilometer road race in about 40 minutes.

   About how many times would your heart beat in one minute at the end of the race? _____

5. How hard does an active heart work in one day? Create, write, and solve a problem using the "fast facts."

   Share your problem with a friend. _____

   _____

   _____

   _____

From the *Arithmetic Teacher*, February 1992

Triangles

LEVELS 5–6

Objectives

Students construct triangles and discover the properties of the segments and angles of various triangles. They also predict and investigate the properties of triangles that tessellate.

Materials

A copy of the "Triangles" activity sheet for each student, paper, pencil, scissors, ruler, protractor, a six-inch-by-six-inch mat, cutouts of various triangles (similar to those furnished on the "Triangles" activity sheet), index cards, glue, and charts (see figs. 1 and 2)

Vocabulary

1. Types of triangles based on sides: *equilateral, isosceles, scalene*

2. Types of triangles based on angles and types of angles: *acute, obtuse, right*

3. Related words: *flip, rotate, vertex, tessellation*

Directions

1. Introduce the activity with a class discussion of triangles. Pictures of objects that have triangular shapes might be helpful. Ask the students to visualize a triangle and have them draw or describe that triangle.

2. Give each student a three-inch-by-five-inch index card and a ruler; ask the students to construct and cut out a triangle to use as a pattern to make a second triangle.

3. Allow the students to compare their triangle with their neighbor's and then show it to the rest of the class. Conduct a discussion of the likenesses and differences of the triangles. To further dis-

cover the likenesses and differences, have the students use a ruler to measure the sides of their triangle. List the students' measurements under the appropriate columns in a chart like that in figure 1; for example, if the sides measure 4, 4, and 4 (all equal), list the measurements under the column head "Equilateral." If each has a different measurement (e.g., 2, 3, 4), list the measurements under "Scalene," and if two sides are equal (e.g., 4, 4, 3), place the measurements under "Isosceles."

4. After all the measurements have been listed, lead the students to determine the meanings of the various names of the triangles. Ask what the triangles in each category have in common.

5. Give the students a protractor to measure all the angles in their triangle. If the students have not used a protractor before, take time to let them discover how it is used. List the angle measures on a chart similar to that in figure 2. If the angle has measure greater than 90 degrees, list it under "Obtuse"; if the angle has measure smaller than 90 degrees, list it as "Acute"; if the angle has measure exactly 90 degrees, enter

FIGURE 1		
Triangles		
Equilateral	Isosceles	Scalene

FIGURE 2				
Categories of Angles				
Triangle	Obtuse	Acute	Right	Sum of degree measures
1				
2				
3				
4				

Prepared by Mary Lou Nevin
Edited by Francis (Skip) Fennell

IDEAS

it under "Right." Help the students determine the characteristics of the different categories of angles. The number of degrees in the measures of the angles of each triangle should be added and recorded on the chart. Ask the students what all the triangles have in common. (Answer: The measures of the angles of each triangle add to 180 degrees.)

6. The students next label the vertices of the copy created in step 2. If the students do not already know the word *vertex*, introduce it at this time. Label the vertices *A*, *B*, and *C* (see fig. 3). The students then cut or tear off angles *A* and *C* and place them next to angle *B*. The measures of the three angles should make a straight line. The teacher can write "$m\angle A + m\angle B + m\angle C = 180°$." Review the various characteristics of the types of triangles, emphasizing that the sum of the measures of the three angles of each triangle is 180 degrees.

7. Give each student a copy of the "Triangles" activity sheet. Refer to the chart. Ask the students to predict which of the triangles can cover the six-inch-by-six-inch mat with no gaps and no overlapping. (Answer: All triangles tessellate.) Have the students complete their activity sheet. Using their original triangle as a model, students should trace and cut out enough triangles to cover the mat. Introduce the word *tessellation* if the students are not familiar with it.

8. After the students have tessellated their triangle, ask them to verify their prediction. Follow up with a discussion of how students made their triangles fit on the paper mat. Introduce or reinforce the terminology *flip* and *rotate*.

FIGURE 3

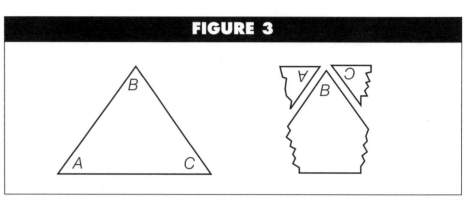

9. Have the students place a dot near a vertex of one of the triangles (see fig. 4) in their pattern and label it "*A*." Ask the following questions: How many adjacent angles are needed so that a straight line is formed? How many degrees are in each of those adjacent angles? Do you observe any other characteristics about your pattern? Next place a dot in the interior of each triangle near the vertex that touches point *A*

(see fig. 5). What shape is made by the dots? How many degrees are in a complete circle?

10. Divide the class into groups of three. Have the students trace many copies of one of their original triangles and use them to solve the following problem:

You are to tile a kitchen floor for a customer who has requested that only triangular tiles be used. The cus-

FIGURE 4

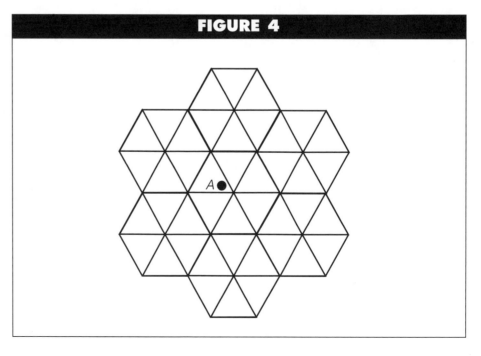

tomer wants a creative-looking floor of several different colors. Experiment with several different patterns before you construct a sample to show to the customer. Once you have decided on a pattern, glue it onto a piece of paper starting at the center of the paper. All tiling starts at the center and then moves out so as to produce a free-flowing design. Think about the design and the colors you will use. All designs will be displayed for the owner to see.

Suggest that students who have difficulty with this project label the vertices of the triangles ($m\angle A + m\angle B + m\angle C = 180$ and $2m\angle A + 2m\angle B + 2m\angle C = 360$).

11. Since the students are only designing the floor, they must write a complete explanation of how the installer should place the tiles on the floor. They should be sure to include any flips or rotations needed to complete the floor. A picture of the design can be included with the directions.

12. After each group has written the installation procedures, the students should exchange directions with members of another group, who then pretend to be the installers and see if they can follow the guidelines for installation.

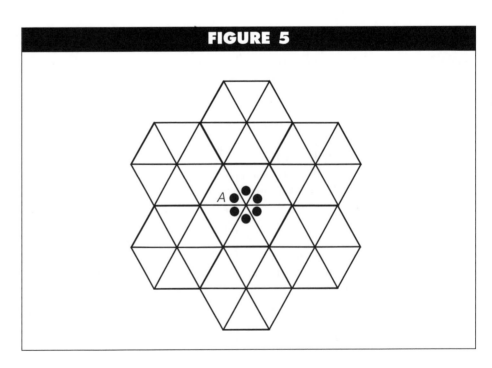

FIGURE 5

Name _____

Triangles

Type of triangle	Will it tessellate?	Measure of each side	Measure of each angle	Type of angles	Did it tessellate?

Types of Triangles That Can Be Used for the "Triangles" Activities

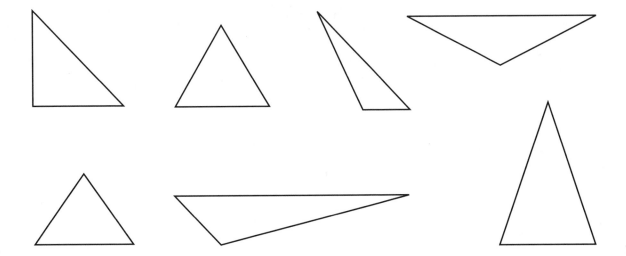

From the *Arithmetic Teacher*, January 1992

IDEAS

Tessellation Combinations

LEVELS 7–8

Objectives

Students use several geometric figures to discover which combinations of figures tessellate. They also discover the combination of figures that fit around a vertex without overlap or gaps.

Materials

Copies of the geometric figures for levels 7–8, a copy of the "Tessellation Combinations" activity sheet for each student, copies of tessellations 1 and 2 for each student, a six-inch-by-six-inch mat, paper, pencil, chart, and a transparency of tessellations

Vocabulary

Names of many of the polygons—*heptagon, hexagon, octagon, triangle, square, trapezoid, parallelogram, rectangle, pentagon*—and *tessellate, flip, rotate*

Directions

1. Discuss the use of geometric figures in our world today.

2. Give the students several sheets of the geometric figures to cut out. (These figures can later be transferred to cardboard to use as pieces in making tessellations.) Discuss the various types of geometric figures. Have the students list the names of the figures in column 1 of the "Geometric Figures" chart on the "Tessellation Combinations" activity sheet. Have them fill in columns 2 and 3 for each figure.

3. After the students have identified the figures and discussed the line segments and angles, give them the six-inch-by-six-inch mat and tell them to use one figure at a time to cover the mat.

No gaps or overlaps are permitted; the figures, however, may extend beyond the side. Before students begin to place the figures on the mat, have them fill in column 4—predictions of whether the figures will tessellate. Then tally their predictions on a chart. Have the students experiment with each figure and verify their predictions. As the students validate their predictions, they should fill in column 5. Introduce a discussion using the following questions: Why did some figures tessellate whereas others did not? From your knowledge of which ones filled the mat, can you predict what other figures tessellate? Did those that filled the mat have anything in common?

Have the students mark one angle, measure the number of degrees in that angle, and record the measure in column 6. They should then measure all other angles that meet that vertex and record their measures in column 6. Finally, they should add the number of degrees in the measures of all the angles around the vertex and enter the total in column 7. In a discussion of the total number of degrees in the angles, help the students deduce that the measures of the angles around the vertex must sum to 360 degrees for the figure to tessellate.

After the students have discovered which single figures tessellate, have them predict which combinations of figures will cover the mat. Make a list of their predictions on the chalkboard, and discuss why they think each combination will tessellate.

4. The students should verify their predictions of which combinations of figures will tessellate. In a follow-up discussion, reinforce that the number of

Prepared by Mary Lou Nevin
Edited by Francis (Skip) Fennell

Applicable Standards

- **Problem Solving**
- **Reasoning**
- **Patterns and Functions**
- **Geometry**

degrees around a point in a tessellation must add to 360.

5. Distribute tessellations 1 and 2. Use an overhead transparency of the two designs to direct the students' attention. Have the students look at the point marked A. Have students use their protractor to measure each of the angles around point A. A summing of the measures of the angles should yield a total of 360 degrees. Once the angle measures have been verified. direct the students' attention to the figures around point A. Using pens of various colors on the overhead projector. trace over one figure at a time, around point A, ask for the number of sides in the figure, and record that number under the tessellation. Continue until all the figures have been identified. Discuss the numbers of sides in the figures that make up the pattern around point A. The combination 4-3-3-4-3, for instance, indicates that two four-sided figures and three three-sided figures compose A tessellation. Mark a different vertex point B, and have students determine the figures around that point.

6. Paired students can take turns marking a vertex on tessellation 1. The other student must state the figures that tessellate around that point. Allow twenty minutes for this activity, then select a student to mark a vertex on the overhead transparency. The other students

Patterns for Figures for the
"Tessellation Combinations" Activities

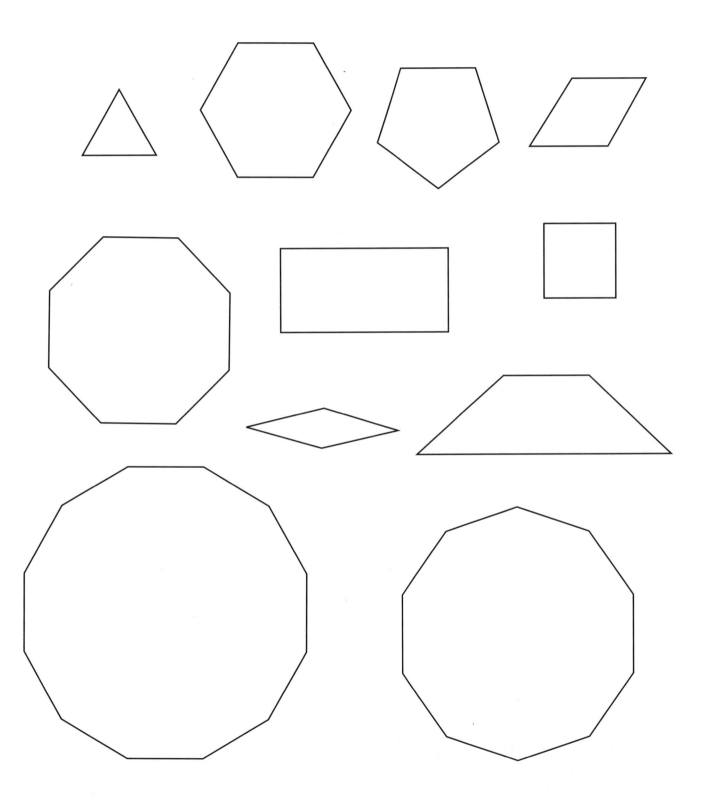

From the *Arithmetic Teacher*, January 1992

must state the figures of the tessellation at that point.

7. Give the students tessellation 2 and direct their attention to the "Geometric Combinations" chart. Students should study the given number combinations and list the figures they think make up the pattern. They then verify their predictions by actually tessellating the figures and list those that actually correspond to the combination. Students should then reflect on why their pre-

dictions were or were not correct.

8. Give groups of four or five students the following problem:

You have been given permission to redesign the floor in your classroom. Since you have been studying tessellations and are experts on figures that will tessellate or can be combined to tessellate, the principal tells you that you may use any figures and sizes of figures for the project. You find the square tiles in the classroom

boring and want to make a change. You decide that since we live in a geometric world, the project would be fun if you used as many geometric figures as possible. As a group you must not only design the floor but also determine the colors of the tiles you will use. Make a design to present to the principal. A secret ballot of all fifth through eighth graders will determine the winning floor design.

Tessellation 1 **Tessellation 2**

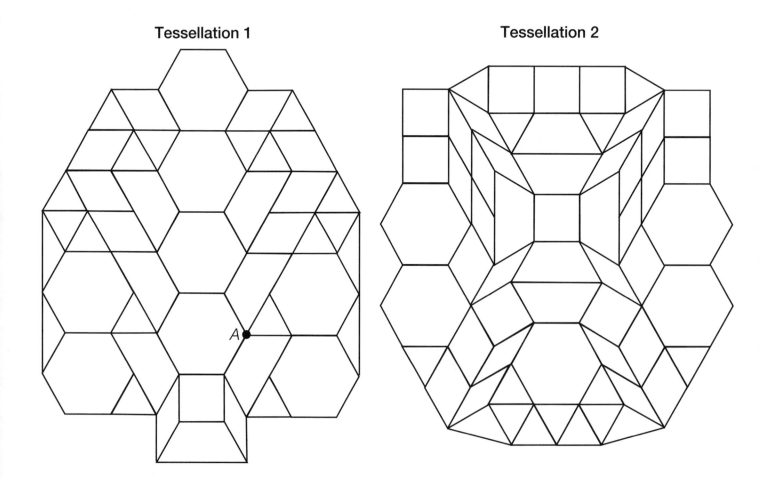

Name _____

Tessellation Combinations

Geometric Figures

1	2	3	4	5	6	7
Figure	Number of line segments	Number of angles	Predict (Will figure tessellate?)	Validate (Did figure tessellate?)	Measure of each angle	Total of degrees around point

Geometric Combinations

Combination	Predicted figures	Actual figures
4-4-6-4		
4-4-4		
4-4-4-4-3		
3-4-3-4		
6-3-4-4		

From the *Arithmetic Teacher*, January 1992

IDEAS

Sports Numbers

LEVELS 5–6

Background

Students are familiar with sports and sporting events. Whole numbers and fractions are used to represent the size of groups or collections and measurements involving lengths, weights, and times in many sporting and game situations. This knowledge can be used to give the students another picture of numbers.

Objectives

Students will be involved in discussing, describing, reading, and writing about whole numbers, decimal or common fractions, or percents.

Directions

1. Reproduce a copy of the activity sheet for each student.

2. Generally discuss the sports-activity sheet with the students. Ask them to tell what they see in each of the scenes on the sheet.

3. Tell the students to look at the pictures and find examples of the use of numbers. Spend enough time talking about the picture and the students'

knowledge of sports so that students describe as many different ways as possible of using numbers. In each instance ask the students to describe how the number is being used. The following observations should be made for each picture:

- Basketball—number of players, position in line-up, dimensions of the court, height of the basket, diameter and circumference of the ball, time remaining in game, fractions of play, team's statistics
- Swimming—lengths of pool or races, swimmers' times, scoring of points, height of diving board
- Indoor track-and-field events—lengths of races, runners' times, weights of objects thrown, lengths of objects thrown
- Board games—dimensions of spaces on various playing boards (checkers, Chinese checkers, etc.), scoring of games

4. Read the directions at the bottom of the activity sheet with the class. The students can then work independently

or in small groups to complete the activities.

Extensions

1. Describe the size of a basketball court, the length of the swimming pool, or the distances of some races in terms of the area or length of the classroom. The students should write a description of the comparison.

2. Have the students research local and world records for selected sports events, for example, the local and world records for the 100-meter race. Have them write a short report of their findings.

Applicable Standards

- **Communication**
- **Connections**
- **Number and Number Relationships**
- **Number Systems and Number Theory**

Prepared by Calvin Irons *and* Rosemary Irons
Edited by Francis (Skip) Fennell

Name _____

Sports Numbers

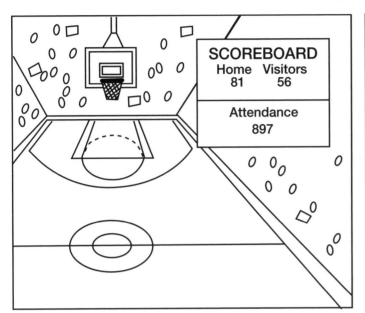

SCOREBOARD

Home   Visitors
81   56

Attendance
897

World record
25-km run
1 hr. 13:55.80

1   2   3   4

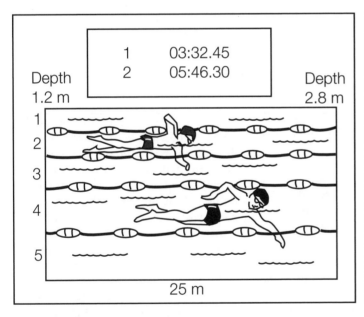

Depth
1.2 m

| 1 | 03:32.45 |
| 2 | 05:46.30 |

Depth
2.8 m

1 2 3 4 5

25 m

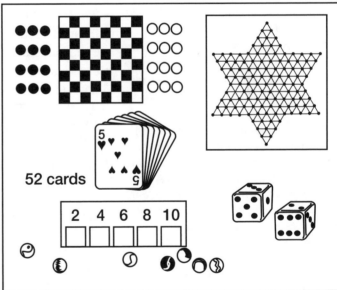

52 cards

2 4 6 8 10

1. For each sports scene, talk about the different ways numbers are used.

2. Think of other ways that numbers are used in sports.

3. Pick one number and write a description of how that number is used. Use the other side if more space is needed.

_____

_____

_____

_____

From the *Arithmetic Teacher*, December 1991

IDEAS

Airport Numbers

LEVELS 7–8

Background

The activities at this level use an airport theme to investigate numbers. Students are encouraged to relate the numbers to familiar situations, for example, to use the dimensions of the classroom to describe an airplane.

Objectives

Students will be involved in discussing, describing, reading, and writing about whole numbers or decimal and common fractions.

Directions

1. Reproduce a copy of the activity sheet for each student.

2. Generally discuss the airport activity sheet with the students. Ask them to tell what they see in each of the pictures and what they think each picture is about.

3. Tell the students to look at the pictures and find examples of the use of numbers. Spend enough time talking about the pictures and students' own knowledge of airports so that students describe as many different ways as possible of using numbers. For each suggestion, ask the students to describe how the number is being used. The following observations should be made for each picture:

- At the check-in counter—number of bags, weight of each bag, dimensions of a bag, cost of tickets
- At the departure gate—time (discuss the 24-hour clock used internationally), departure times of other flights, dates (discuss the different conventions—month/day/year and day/month/year), flight numbers, seat-assignment numbers
- Runway—identifications of the airplane and runway
- Airplane statistics—measurement of various attributes (length, width, height, capacity)

4. Ask the students to work in groups to write descriptions of as wide a variety of uses of numbers as possible in other areas of the airport. They should include numbers in the following forms:

- Whole numbers
- Decimal fractions
- Common fractions
- Percents

5. The students can work independently or in small groups to complete the activities given in the directions at the bottom of the activity sheet.

Extensions

1. Obtain an airline-flight schedule. Ask the students to study it and find as many different uses of numbers as possible.

2. Have the students collect information about the distances of various routes flown within the United States and internationally from the United States. Have the students research the distance of the shortest commercial flight (currently 25 miles—between Green Bay, Wisconsin, and Appleton, Wisconsin) and the longest commercial flight (currently 7483 miles—between Los Angeles, California, and Sydney, Australia).

3. Have the students use the airline information they collected in extension 2 to create problems, for example, "How many trips between Green Bay and Appleton equal one trip between Los Angeles and Sydney?"

4. The number on the runway, multiplied by 10, corresponds to the compass heading of the airplane as it is landing. For example, on runway 32 the compass heading as the plane lands is 320 (an L or R after the number indicates the left or right runway, respectively). Explore further the topic of compass headings. The students should write a short report about the information they find. The students might want to find out the range of numbers of compass headings (0 to 360), the numbers that correspond to the points of the compass (90, or 09, on the runway is east; 18, or 180, is south, etc.), and the reason that the number 360 was chosen for the number of degrees in a circle (the ancients thought that the complete cycle of one year contained 360 days).

Prepared by Calvin Irons *and* Rosemary Irons
Edited by Francis (Skip) Fennell

Airport Numbers

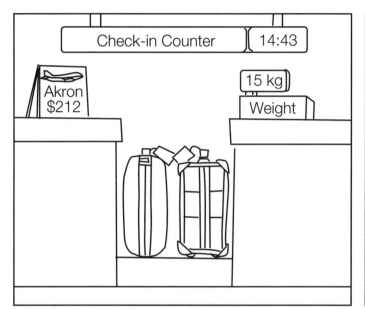

Check-in Counter   14:43

Akron
$212

15 kg
Weight

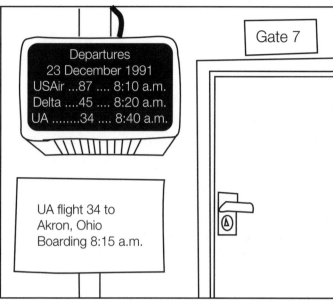

Gate 7

Departures
23 December 1991
USAir ...87 .... 8:10 a.m.
Delta ....45 .... 8:20 a.m.
UA ....34 .... 8:40 a.m.

UA flight 34 to
Akron, Ohio
Boarding 8:15 a.m.

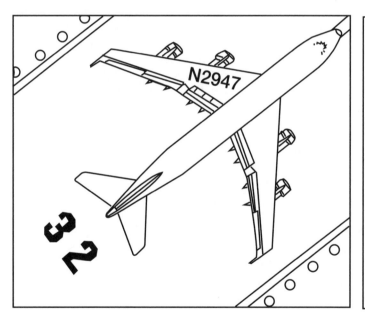

N2947

32

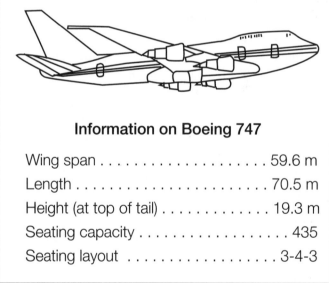

Information on Boeing 747

Wing span . . . . 59.6 m
Length . . . . 70.5 m
Height (at top of tail) . . . . 19.3 m
Seating capacity 435
Seating layout 3-4-3

1. Research to find more information on airplanes of other sizes.
2. Write about the information you discovered.
3. Write a description to compare airplanes of different sizes. Use the other side if more space is needed.

_____

_____

_____

_____

From the *Arithmetic Teacher*, December 1991

Make a Puzzle

LEVELS 5–6

Background

In this activity, students are involved in experimenting to cut a rectangular region into several pieces. The pieces are used as a puzzle to make the original rectangular region or some other specified figure. For example, a four-centimeter-by-nine-centimeter rectangle is cut into four pieces (2 triangular regions and 2 rectangular regions) and rearranged to make a square region. The students first decide how to cut the original rectangular region and determine the directions for constructing the new figure. They then write the directions for rearranging the pieces.

Objectives

1. To reconstruct a rectangular region that has been cut into pieces and describe the result

2. To develop directions for a game involving figures cut from a rectangular region

3. To construct a new figure from pieces cut from a rectangular region

Materials

1. A copy of the "Make a Puzzle" activity sheet for each student

2. Construction paper for each pair of students

3. A pair of scissors for each student

4. A ruler for each student

5. Paste for each student

Directions

1. Reproduce a copy of the activity sheet for each student.

2. Read the directions on the activity sheet together with the students. Discuss the sample puzzle shown at the top of the page. Clarify any questions the students might have. Make sure the students understand that they can begin with any size of rectangle and that they should carefully work out what they are going to do before they start.

3. Have the students work in pairs. Give each pair of students a sheet of construction paper. Have the pairs work together to plan how they will construct their puzzle. Each student in the pair can cut out a rectangular region of the same dimensions as the rectangular region in their puzzle.

4. The students should cut up both rectangular regions to make the puzzle pieces. One of the cut-up rectangular regions should be pasted on an activity sheet. The students should also write the directions on the activity sheet.

5. Have the students exchange the activity sheets and puzzle pieces and try to construct the new figure from each other's pieces.

6. Have each pair of students explain to the whole class what they did to make their puzzles. Encourage the students to give full explanations of how they determined the size of the smaller pieces.

Applicable Standards

- **Communication**
- **Geometry**
- **Measurement**

Extensions

1. Repeat the activity completely, but have the students cut out more (or fewer) pieces in the puzzles.

2. Challenge the students to cut and rearrange a rectangular region to make a new rectangular region with different dimensions. They could construct a new rectangular region by cutting the original rectangular region into two figures, three figures, or four figures.

Prepared by Calvin Irons *and* Rosemary Irons

Edited by Francis (Skip) Fennell

Name _____

Make a Puzzle

Changing a Rectangular Region into a Square Region

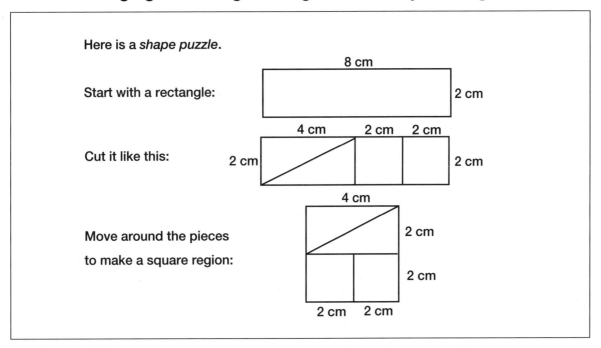

Here is a *shape puzzle*.

Start with a rectangle:

8 cm
2 cm

Cut it like this:

4 cm   2 cm   2 cm
2 cm   2 cm

Move around the pieces
to make a square region:

4 cm
2 cm
2 cm
2 cm   2 cm

Start with a rectangle of any size.
Cut your rectangular region into four to six pieces to make a new figure.

Paste your new figure here.

Write directions on how to use your puzzle.

_____
_____
_____
_____

From the *Arithmetic Teacher*, November 1991

Triangular Regions Make Many Figures

LEVELS 7–8

Background

In this activity, students cut a rectangular region into twelve identical triangular regions. They then experiment to rearrange the triangular regions to construct new figures. Throughout the investigation, the students describe what they are doing. The teacher should encourage discussion leading to observations about the area of the figures and to predictions about what might occur as the number of triangular regions cut from the same rectangular region increases.

Objectives

1. To construct a new figure from a rectangular region cut into twelve congruent triangular regions and describe in oral and written form the process and the result

2. To investigate informally the area properties of a rectangle and a circle

Materials

• A copy of the activity sheet "Triangular Regions Make Many Figures" for each student

• A sheet of construction paper for each pair of students

• A pair of scissors for each pair of students

• A ruler for each pair of students

• Paste for each pair of students

Directions

1. Reproduce a copy of the activity sheet for each student.

2. Read the directions on the activity sheet together with the students. Clari-

Prepared by Calvin Irons *and* Rosemary Irons
Edited by Francis (Skip) Fennell

fy any questions the students might have. The students should measure the rectangle at the top of the sheet to make sure that the length is three times the width.

3. Have the students work in pairs. Give each pair a sheet of construction paper. The students can work together to complete the activity sheet. Encourage them to try several different figures before they decide on the one they will paste on the sheet. Also encourage the class to produce a variety of different figures.

4. Ask each pair of students to explain what they wrote. In the discussion, have the students focus on the area of each new figure and ask them to tell how they could find the area of the new figure.

5. Look at the twelve-sided polygonal region called a *dodecagon* (see fig. 1), made by arranging the twelve triangular regions so that their smallest angles meet at the same point without overlapping. Ask the students to refer to the original rectangular region and tell—

a) how to find its area and

b) how and why the area of the rectangular region relates to the area of a circle.

Extensions

1. Repeat the steps on the activity sheet, but have the students cut in the same manner the original rectangular region into twenty-four triangular regions. Have the students experiment to make a twenty-four-sided polygonal region.

2. Ask the students to construct a rectangle having a length that is two times, four times, or five times its width. They

should then cut out twelve triangular regions in a manner similar to that shown on the activity sheet. Have the students try to arrange the triangular regions to make a twelve-sided polygonal region. Discuss what happens. (*Note:* When the length of the rectangle is more or less than 3.14 times the width, it is difficult to make a polygonal region without gaps or overlaps.) Discuss what happens and why gaps or overlaps occur.

FIGURE 1

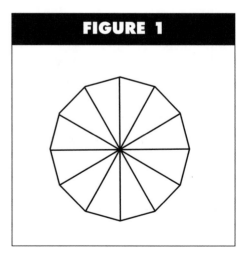

Name _____

Triangular Regions Make Many Figures

Cut a rectangular region whose length is three times its width into twelve triangular regions as shown below.

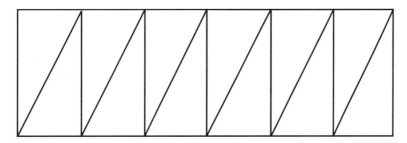

Rearrange the triangular regions to make a new figure.

Paste the new figure here.

Write what you did to make the new figure.

_____

_____

_____

_____

From the *Arithmetic Teacher*, November 1991

Name Your Tune

LEVELS 5–6

Background

The activities at this level focus on studying information displayed in picture graphs that report the sales of records, tapes, and compact discs for one week at a music store. The students are asked to discuss and describe the information and to explain the numbers sold in each category. They are asked to defend their explanation.

Objectives

To describe, explain, and make written predictions about information displayed in picture graphs

Directions

1. Reproduce a copy of the activity sheet for each student.

2. Have the students read the title of the graph and interpret the rebus information. The students should give their interpretation of the information in the graph and each of its sections. Ask the students to explain—

- why the store might want to know this information for different types of music rather than the sales as a whole;

- what might happen if they looked at the storewide sales for the various formats rather than the separate types of music.

3. Discuss how the store might have constructed the graph. Have the students read the information for the different types of music and formats. The students could write the number of sales on each graph.

4. Read and discuss question 1. In the discussion have the students tell why they think—

- the total sales vary for the different types of music. What do the differences imply about the interests of clients, the location of the store, prices, and so on?

- the total sales vary for the different formats;

- the sales vary for the various formats according to the different types of music.

Allow enough time in the discussion for every student in the group to offer a suggestion. The students can also ask their own questions about the graph and select other members of the class to answer.

5. The students work in pairs to complete question 2. Ask the students to share their explanations.

Applicable Standards

- **Communication**
- **Statistics**

Extensions

1. In pairs, have the students evaluate the use of a picture graph to show the sales at the music store. The students should write what type of graph—bar, scatterplot, picture, or pie—they think is the best for showing the information and why that graph is better than any other type.

2. Have the students work together to plan the music store's future purchases. Tell the students the store plans to order 5000 units. The students can work in small groups to decide the number that should be ordered for each type of music and each format.

Family activity

See "Gathering Graphs" on page 126.

Prepared by Calvin Irons *and* Rosemary Irons
Edited by Francis (Skip) Fennell

Name

Name Your Tune

Music Store's October Sales

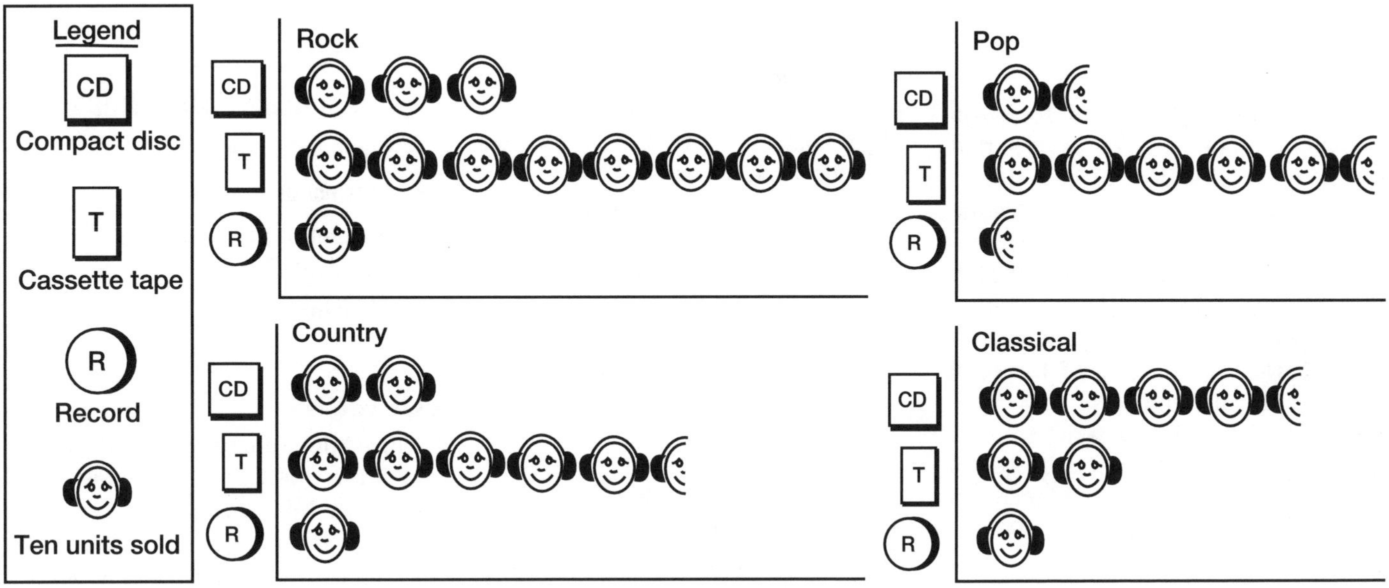

Legend

CD — Compact disc

T — Cassette tape

R — Record

(face) — Ten units sold

Rock

CD: (3 faces)
T: (8 faces)
R: (1 face)

Pop

CD: (2 faces)
T: (7 faces)
R: (1 face)

Country

CD: (2 faces)
T: (6 faces)
R: (1 face)

Classical

CD: (4 faces)
T: (2 faces)
R: (1 face)

Examine the graphs and use them to answer the following:

1. How do the graphs vary? _____

2. Are tapes more or less popular than records or CDs? _____

3. Were more rock tapes sold than country-music tapes? _____

4. How many CDs were sold? _____

5. Are tapes, CDs, or records most popular? _____ Explain your answer. _____

   _____

6. Which type of music is most popular? _____

   How do you know? _____

7. Write and answer your own questions based on the information about the store's sales. _____

   _____

   _____

8. Write some reasons for the variations in the popularity of CDs, tapes, and records for the different types of music. _____

   _____

   _____

From the *Arithmetic Teacher*, October 1991

History of Populations

Background

The activities at this level focus on studying a series of pie graphs that report the population of the United States and of selected states—Massachusetts, New York, and Pennsylvania—in fifty-year intervals from 1800 to 1950. The students are asked to discuss and describe the information and to explain why the percent of the total population changed for the three states. They are asked to write a justification for their explanation. The 1990 census data required for problem 6 can be found at the bottom of the family-activity sheet on page 127.

Objectives

To describe, explain, and make written predictions from information displayed in pie graphs

Directions

1. Reproduce a copy of the activity sheet for each student.

2. Have the students describe what they see in the graphs. Ask them to give an explanation of the information shown in the graphs. Ask the students to—

• describe the information in each pie graph and

• explain what steps would have been followed to construct the graphs.

3. Record the following information on the chalkboard. Then ask the students to figure out the population of the three states for the four dates.

Population of the United States
(nearest million)

1800	4 000 000
1850	23 000 000
1900	76 000 000
1950	170 000 000

4. Discuss the following questions:

• How do the percents for each of the three states and the other states change from one graph to the other?

• What was happening to the population for the three states throughout the time span covered by the graphs?

• Did the percents for the three states decrease from one fifty-year period to the next?

• Why do you think the percent for New York increased between 1800 and 1850?

5. Have the students work in pairs to complete question 1. Explain to the students that they can write a general explanation looking at all the statistics or select one state and study the information for that state in the four pie graphs. Ask the students to share their explanations.

Applicable Standards

• **Communication**

• **Connections**

• **Number and Number Relationships**

• **Statistics**

Extensions

1. Have the students find out population information for other states that existed in 1800 for each of the years shown in the pie graphs on the worksheet—1800, 1850, 1900, and 1950. Ask the students to calculate the percents of the population of each of those years for each state. Then they can study the percents to check if the general trend was similar to the trend shown in the pie graphs.

2. Find out the current population of Massachusetts, New York, Pennsylvania, and the United States. Construct a pie graph to represent the population information. Determine if the general trend shown on the activity sheet continues. Ask the students to predict what a pie graph for the three states and "Other states" will look like in the year 2000.

Family activity

See "Gathering Graphs" on page 126.

Prepared by Calvin Irons *and* Rosemary Irons
Edited by Francis (Skip) Fennell

Name _____

History of Populations

Populations of Massachusetts, New York, Pennsylvania, and the Other States in Fifty-Year Intervals

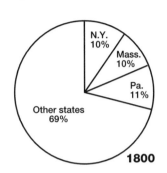
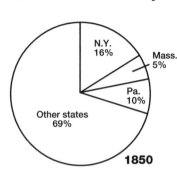
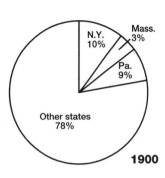
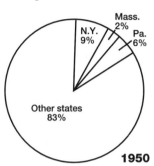

Review the circle graphs, then answer the following:

1. What percent of the population of the United States did the states of New York, Pennsylvania, and Massachusetts contain in 1800?_____ Did this percent increase or decrease in 1850, 1900, and 1950?_____ Explain your answer. _____

2. Which of the three states specified on the graph had the largest population in—

    1800? _____ 1850? _____ 1900? _____ 1950? _____

    Which of the three would you predict will have the largest population in the year 2000?_____

3. Which state's percent of the total population of the United States has decreased the most from 1800 to 1950? _____ How much? _____ How do you know? _____

4. How many states represented the "other states" portion of the graph in—

    1800? _____ 1900? _____ 1850? _____ 1950? _____

    What resource did you use to help answer this question? _____

5. Write an explanation for the changes in the percent of the population in each of the three states.

    _____

6. Using the 1990 census data given on the "Gathering Graphs" family-activity sheet, predict the populations of New York, Pennsylvania, Massachusetts, and "Other states" for the year 2000:

    New York _____   Pennsylvania _____

    Massachusetts _____   Other states _____

7. Using your state and your neighboring states, construct a circle graph representing the percent of the total U.S. population represented by your state, your neighboring states, and "Other states."

From the *Arithmetic Teacher*, October 1991

IDEAS

Heights of Students in Our Class

LEVELS 4–7

Background

In this activity students collect data and then construct a box-and-whisker plot to display the results. The activity sheet actually presents a sequence for setting up a box-and-whisker plot. Additional information on box-and-whisker plots can be found in *Developing Graph Comprehension: Elementary and Middle School Activities* by Frances R. Curcio (Reston, Va.: NCTM, 1989, pp. 47–48).

Objective

To display and interpret data using a box-and-whisker plot

Directions

1. Reproduce a copy of the activity sheet for each student.

2. Have the students find the height, in centimeters, of eleven students, including themselves.

3. Have the student order the heights from least to greatest by plotting them on the number line. Have them plot each height with an X.

4. Ask the students to determine the middle height of the eleven heights plotted. Ask why the middle height is the sixth height. Explain that the middle height is called the *median*.

5. Ask the students to determine where the third and ninth heights fall. Indicate that these points represent the first and third quartiles, respectively. Ask the students to explain why this result is so. Have the students draw a box above the area delineated by the third to ninth heights. Then have them draw a verti-

cal line segment inside the box denoting the sixth height (see fig. 1).

6. Ask the students to draw a line segment from each edge of the box to the smallest and largest heights. These lines represent the "whiskers" of a box-and-whisker plot. Ask the students why they think these line segments are called *whiskers*.

7. Have the students complete items 7–9. These questions help the students understand how to interpret the box-and-whisker plot. Discuss the responses to these items with the class.

Answers

1, 3, 5, 6, 7, and 8. Answers will vary.

2. The sixth height is the middle height.

4. The third and ninth heights have two heights between them and the sixth, or median, height.

9. Eleven is a convenient number to use because it facilitates locating the median and the first and third quartiles, since they are actual heights. The plot would be harder to draw with ten heights, since the students would need to average the two middle scores to compute the median.

Applicable Standards

- **Statistics**
- **Measurement**

Extensions

1. Have the students arrange their height data using a stem-and-leaf plot (see fig. 2). Use the tens and hundreds digits as the stem. For information on constructing stem-and-leaf plots, see Curcio (1989, 46-48).

2. Have the students determine the mean, median, and mode for the heights.

Extension answers

Answers will vary.

FIGURE 2

Example of a stem-and-leaf plot involving the same eleven heights

```
13 | 0 5 7
14 | 0 2 3 5
15 | 0 2 8
16 | 5
```

Prepared by Dianne Bankard *and* Francis (Skip) Fennell
Edited by Francis (Skip) Fennell

FIGURE 1

Example of a box-and-whisker plot involving eleven heights

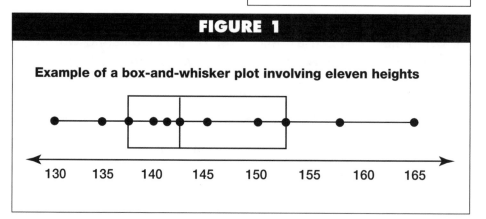

Heights of Students in Our Class

Directions: Find the height (in cm) of any ten students in your classroom. Record the heights in order from greatest to least. Include your own height so that eleven heights are recorded.

Name	Height		Name	Height
1. _____	_____	7. _____	_____	
2. _____	_____	8. _____	_____	
3. _____	_____	9. _____	_____	
4. _____	_____	10. _____	_____	
5. _____	_____	11. _____	_____	
6. _____	_____			

Making a Box-and-Whisker Plot

Follow the directions to display the height data as a box-and-whisker plot.

1. Using an X for each height, record your data on the number line at the bottom of the page.

2. Find the middle of the eleven heights recorded. In which place is it in the ordered sequence? _____ What is the height? _____

3. Find the third least and ninth least heights. What are they?
_____ and _____

4. How are the third and ninth least heights related to the middle height? _____
_____

5. Draw vertical line segments through the third and ninth heights, then connect the ends of the line segments to form a box. Draw a vertical line segment in the box to show the middle height. You have created a box plot.

6. Draw line segments from the middle of the edges of the box (3rd and 9th heights) to the least and greatest heights. The line segments represent the "whiskers" in a box-and-whisker plot.

7. Is the middle height closer to that for the third-shortest or third-tallest student? _____
How do you know? _____

8. Which height—the greatest or the least—is closer to the left end of the box? _____
To the right end of the box? _____ How do you know? _____
_____

9. Why was it fairly easy to do a box-and-whisker plot with eleven people? _____
_____

Height in Centimeters

0	15	30	45	60	75	90	105	120	135	150	165	180

From the *Arithmetic Teacher*, September 1991

IDEAS

About Our Class

Background

This activity involves the collection and analysis of data about a student's family and his or her personal interests. Students determine the arithmetic mean and represent data using percent.

Objective

To collect and interpret data using mean, range, and percent

Directions

1. Reproduce a copy of the activity sheet for each student.

2. Have the students complete survey questions *a–g*. Discuss the results as a class. Ask the students to think of a way to represent this information. Consider having groups of students construct a table to display the class's data for all responses to questions *a–g*.

3. Have the students use a calculator to determine the mean number of people living in each house. Find the sum of the people in all the houses and divide this sum by the number of houses. Define *range* as the difference between the numbers of people in the smallest and largest household, then ask for the range of the household sizes.

4. Ask the class to report the total number and mean of the number of cars. Then ask how students could determine the percent of families that have at least one car. (Make a table showing the numbers of families with various numbers of cars, and then determine the percent of families with at least one car by dividing the number of families with one or more cars by the total number of families.)

5. Have the class discuss the mean number of calculators in the families and the percent of families that have *at least one* calculator in their home. Remind the students that if they have at least one, they could have more than one.

6. Ascertain the favorite activity for the class. Ask how this answer was determined.

7. Discuss the difference between the number of times the most common favorite and the second most common favorite TV shows were mentioned. The greater the difference between the two numbers, the greater is the likelihood that the favorite will still be the favorite in another sample.

8. Discuss the completed graphs and questions from the class.

Answers

Answers will vary.

Extensions

1. Have the students work in groups to create a way to organize the class's responses to each of the survey questions. Ask the students to display their data for the class.

Extension answers

Answers will vary.

Prepared by Dianne Bankard *and* Francis (Skip) Fennell
Edited by Francis (Skip) Fennell

Name _____

About Our Class

Directions: Answer the following questions. Use this information to complete the class composite.

(a) How many people live in your house (include yourself!)? _____

(b) How many cars does your family have?_____

(c) How many calculators does your family have? _____

(d) What is your favorite activity? _____

(e) What is your favorite participation sport?_____

(f) What is your favorite spectator sport? _____

(g) What is your favorite TV show? _____

Class Composite

1. What is the mean number of people living in the houses of the students in our class?_____
   What is the range? _____

2. Our class has _____ cars. The mean number of cars owned by the students' families is _____.
   What percent of the families have at least one car? _____

3. _____ percent of our class have at least one calculator in the home. The mean number of calculators owned by the students' families is _____.

4. Our class's most common favorite activity is _____.

5. What is the difference between the number of times the most common favorite and the second most common favorite TV shows were mentioned by the class?
   _____ If you took the same survey in another class, would the order of results be the same? _____ Why or why not? _____

From the *Arithmetic Teacher*, September 1991

Television Commercials

LEVELS 3–6

Objective
Students collect data on the types of products advertised during children's television programs. The data are collected at home, analyzed with a group of students, and displayed as a bar graph.

Materials
- A copy of the "Television Data Sheet" on page 105 for each student
- A copy of the "Television Commercials" activity sheet for each student
- A copy of a weekly television-program guide for each group

Directions
1. Give students the following situation, ask the accompanying questions, and then discuss possible answers.

Situation

Your brother goes with you to the grocery store to buy cereal. You pick out a nutritious cereal, but your brother wants to buy a different brand that was advertised on a children's television program. Your brother's choice costs more and is not as nutritious.

Questions

- Why does your brother want the different brand?
- Why did the manufacturer of your brother's choice of cereal advertise on a children's program?

2. As a class, brainstorm various types of products that are typically advertised during children's television programs (toys, cereals, gum, children's movies and videos, etc.). List the suggested products on the chalkboard.

3. Place students in groups of three to five students. Discuss group behaviors: help one another, disagree in an agreeable way, listen to others in your group, take turns.

4. Distribute copies of "Television Commercials." For item 1, ask students to study the list on the chalkboard and guess, individually or as a group, what type of product is most frequently advertised during children's programs.

5. Distribute copies of the "Television Data Sheet." Note the data on the nature of advertising for children's Saturday television programs in 1971. Have students compare their guesses with the data from 1971. Discuss whether they think the types of products advertised on Saturday children's shows have changed since then or stayed about the same.

6. Have the groups discuss different methods for checking their guesses and then share their ideas with the class. Perhaps the most obvious method is to have students keep a log of television programs they watch and list the products advertised for each program. Encourage students to discuss how to record commercials that are repeated during a program. To make sure all

children's programs are viewed, students should decide on which day or days they want to survey the programs and during what hours of the day. Teachers may want to have different groups survey different days or different channels on the same day. Students should also decide whether they want to collect data only on Saturday (for comparison with the 1971 data) or to extend the survey to other days. The groups can use television-program guides to decide who is to view which programs for their logs.

7. After students have collected their data, direct them to work in groups. First they will need to sort the products by type and then make a group bar graph to display their combined data.

Answers
Answers will vary. A completed graph is shown in figure 1.

Family activity
See "Television at Home" on page 128.

Edited and prepared by Sharon L. Young

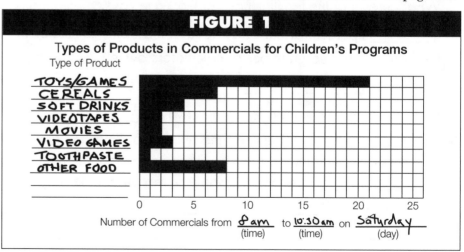

FIGURE 1

Types of Products in Commercials for Children's Programs

Type of Product

TOYS/GAMES
CEREALS
SOFT DRINKS
VIDEOTAPES
MOVIES
VIDEO GAMES
TOOTHPASTE
OTHER FOOD

0   5   10   15   20   25

Number of Commercials from _8 am_ to _10:30 am_ on _Saturday_
(time)   (time)   (day)

Television Commercials

Work in a group.

1. Make a guess. What type of product, such as toys, cars, and food, do you think is advertised most often during children's programs?

_____

2. Find a way to check your guess. Make a bar graph to display your data.

Types of Products in Commercials for Children's Programs

Type of Product

TOYS

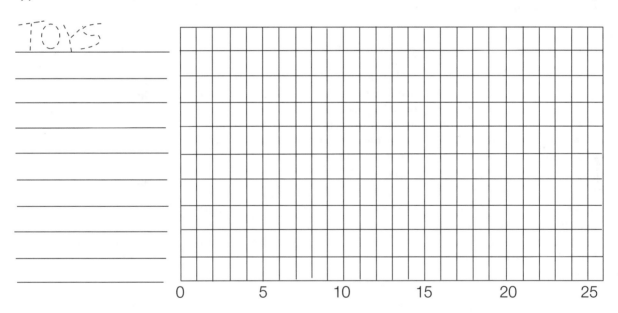

Number of Commercials from _____ to _____ on _____
(time)   (time)   (day)

3. Compare your results to the 1971 data on the "Television Data Sheet." Tell how commercial products advertised on children's television have changed since 1971 and how they have stayed the same.

_____

_____

_____

_____

_____

From the *Arithmetic Teacher*, May 1991

IDEAS

Television Viewing Time

LEVELS 4–8

Objective

Students keep logs of their television viewing times for one week. They then compute their weekly viewing totals, as well as averages for other groups of students, and compare their data with those from Nielsen reports.

Materials

- A copy of the "Television Data Sheet" on page 105 for each student
- A copy of the "Television Viewing Time" activity sheet for each student

Directions

1. Ask students such questions as these, discussing their responses as a class:

- During a typical school week, do you think you spend more time watching television or going to school?
- What data would you need to find out?
- What could you do to obtain the data?

2. Place students in groups of three to five students. Discuss group behaviors: help one another, disagree in an agreeable way, listen to others in your group, take turns.

3. Distribute copies of "Television Viewing Time." Have students make guesses for item 1 and then discuss item 2. Direct each group to discuss various methods for keeping a log of the time they view television. In addition to noting the time, students could also note specific programs they watch and whether the program appears on a cable channel or a network channel.

4. After one week of log keeping, have students once again meet in their groups to share their data. Direct the groups to find a group average of the viewing time for each day and for the total week. Have the groups report their findings and make comparisons among the groups. Then have the students combine the data for the entire class and determine the class's average for both the daily viewing time and the total viewing time for the week. (Caution: when computing the average for the entire class, do not average the group averages. Instead, find the total viewing time for the entire class and then compute the average using that total.)

5. Distribute copies of the "Television Data Sheet." Discuss with students the table titled "Weekly viewing activity by age, 1989," noting the data for your students' age group. In item 4 of the activity sheet, students write about comparisons they make between their viewing times and those reported in the data sheet.

6. Students can determine the total time they are in school and compare those data with their television-viewing-time data to answer the question posed in item 1.

Extensions

1. Make a line graph using the data on forty years of household viewing time from the "Television Data Sheet." Write some conclusions about the changes in viewing time over the years.

Applicable Standards

- **Communication**
- **Computation and Estimation**

2. Conduct a mock "rating" of programs. Television ratings have nothing to do with the quality of the program; they are an estimate of how many televisions are tuned to a program. For example, since 92.1 million U.S. households have television sets, a rating of 20 represents an estimate that 20 percent, or 18.4 million, of those households viewed that program. Students could collect data for a given day and time regarding which programs their televisions are tuned to. Figure 1 shows hypothetical data for a class of thirty students.

3. Discuss with students the data on viewing-time totals and achievement-test scores given in the data sheet, eliciting from students the observation that an inverse relationship exists between the amount of television-viewing time and the achievement-test scores.

Family activity

See "Television at Home" on page 128.

Edited and prepared by Sharon L. Young

FIGURE 1

Television ratings for Monday, 5:00–6:00 P.M.

Program	Number of households watching	Rating
"Cartoon Capers"	15	50
"Afterschool News"	3	10
"The Family Next Door"	6	20

Note: Six of the thirty television sets were not turned on at this hour.

Name _____

Television Viewing Time

Work in a group.

1. Make some guesses. How many hours per week do you think—

   • you spend watching television?

   _____

   • students your age spend watching television?

   _____

2. Keep a log of your television viewing times for one week. Record daily and weekly totals in the chart.

3. Find the average daily and weekly viewing times for your group of students and then for your class and record them in the chart.

Television Viewing-Time Totals for One Week (in Minutes)

Day of week	My viewing time	Group average	Class average
Monday			
Tuesday			
Wednesday			
Thursday			
Friday			
Saturday			
Sunday			
Total for week			

4. Compare the three totals for the week (yours and those for the group's average and the class's average) with the data on weekly viewing activity from the "Television Data Sheet." To compare, you must convert your data in minutes to their equivalents in hours and minutes. Write about the comparisons.

_____

_____

_____

From the *Arithmetic Teacher,* May 1991

Fingerprint Detective

LEVELS 4–8

Objective

Students use fingerprint characteristics to prove that two fingerprints match.

Materials

- A copy of the "Fingerprint Data Sheet" on page 107 for each student
- A copy of the "Fingerprint Detective" activity sheet for each student
- A magnifying glass for each pair of students

Directions

1. Distribute copies of the "Fingerprint Data Sheet" and discuss the seven fingerprint characteristics with the students. See the teaching notes under "About the Fingerprint Data Sheet" on page 106 for a description of these characteristics.

2. Distribute copies of the "Fingerprint Detective" activity sheet. Study the three labeled characteristics of the fingerprint at the top of the sheet. Discuss with students that similarity of patterns is not the only match used to identify fingerprints. They have to match on many different characteristics. The comparison must show the location of the characteristics, as shown in figure 1. For example, the information that two fingerprints each had eight bifurcations would not be sufficient to determine that the fingerprints matched, since all eight of those bifurcations would have to be in the same position on each fingerprint for the prints to be identical. To use fingerprint matches as evidence in court, some states require as few as eight separate matching characteristics, whereas other states require twelve, fifteen, or eighteen matching characteristics as proof that the prints match.

3. Each pair of students should have

Edited and prepared by Sharon L. Young

100

a magnifying glass. If not enough glasses are available, the teacher may have to alternate this activity with another and extend it over several days.

Extension

Have each student make two copies of her or his right thumbprint on different slips of white paper. Place students in groups. Have each student place one of his or her right thumbprints in a paper bag. Next, have a student pick one of the thumbprints from the bag and compare it to the fingerprints that the students are still holding. Prove whose thumbprint was drawn by finding twelve matching characteristics.

Answers

1. Maria took a piece of her own birth-

Applicable Standards

- **Problem Solving**
- **Connections**
- **Patterns and Functions**

day cake before the party started!

2. Answers will vary, since students may identify characteristics different from those given here. A sample answer is given in figure 2. The corresponding matching characteristics are these:

1. Bifurcation	2. Ending ridge
3. Enclosure	4. Bifurcation
5. Bifurcation	6. Bifurcation
7. Bifurcation	8. Ending ridge
9. Bifurcation	10. Dot
11. Bifurcation	12. Hook

FIGURE 1

Comparison of fingerprints

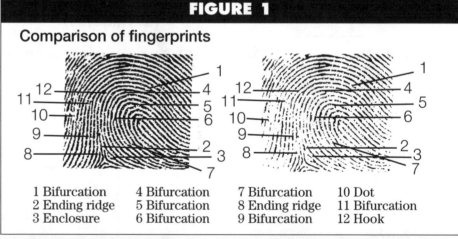

1 Bifurcation	4 Bifurcation
2 Ending ridge	5 Bifurcation
3 Enclosure	6 Bifurcation

7 Bifurcation	10 Dot
8 Ending ridge	11 Bifurcation
9 Bifurcation	12 Hook

FIGURE 2

Twelve characteristics that match Maria's thumbprint

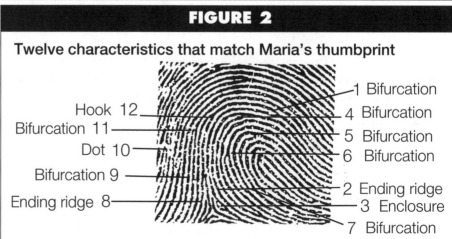

Fingerprint Detective

1. Work with a partner to find out who took a piece of Maria's cake before the birthday party!

Bifurcation

Ending ridge

Enclosure

Enlarged right thumbprint lifted from cake knife

_____
(Name of suspect)

Prove your suspicion by finding and marking at least twelve characteristics of the suspect's thumbprint that match those of the thumbprint found on the cake knife. Three matching characteristics have already been identified. Use the "Fingerprint Data Sheet" to help you.

Mom

Dad

Maria

David

2. List twelve matching characteristics.

1. Bifurcation

2. Ending ridge

3. Enclosure

4. _____

5. _____

6. _____

7. _____

8. _____

9. _____

10. _____

11. _____

12. _____

From the *Arithmetic Teacher*, March 1991

Data Sheets

IDEAS

About the

Television Data Sheet

Directions

This data sheet should be duplicated and used with two of the class-activity sheets and the take-home family-activity sheet. The following information will help teachers and students interpret the television data.

1. The data collected from the A. C. Nielsen Company include cable-channel viewing. Additional data are available from Nielsen Media Research, 1290 Avenue of the Americas, New York, NY 10104. The data for viewing time per television-owning household include the total time a television is being viewed in a particular household, although that total time may comprise viewing times of several different people watching at various times of the day.

2. The data for viewing-time totals and achievement-test scores are the result of a 1982 study conducted by the California State Department of Education, which evaluated 500 000 sixth and twelfth graders.

3. *Prime time* is defined as 8:00 P.M.–11:00 P.M. except in central-time and mountain-time zones, where it is 7:00 P.M.–10:00 P.M.

4. The data on the distribution of program elements in children's Saturday programs in 1971 include two types of commercial announcements: those advertising products or publicizing political candidates and those promoting other programs, usually on the same network or channel. Noncommercial announcements include public-service announcements and station identification.

Bibliography

A. C. Nielsen Company. *Nielsen Report on Television 1990*. New York: Nielsen Media Research, 1990.

Barcus, F. Earle, with Rachel Wolkin. *Children's Television: An Analysis of Programming and Advertising*. New York: Praeger Publishers, 1977.

Bryant, Jennings, ed. *Television and the American Family*. Hillsdale, N.J.: Lawrence Erlbaum Associates, 1990.

Kaplan, Don. *Television and the Classroom*. White Plains, N.Y.: Knowledge Industry Publications, 1986.

Extension

Send home a copy of the "Television Data Sheet," along with a copy of "Television at Home," the family-activity sheet on page 128. Ask students to record the results of the home activities and then share the results with the class.

Television Data Sheet

Weekly viewing activity by age, 1989*

Group	Average time per week
Females	
12–17	21 h. 16 min.
18–34	29 h. 16 min.
35–54	31 h. 28 min.
55+	41 h. 19 min.
Males	
12–17	22 h. 18 min.
18–34	24 h. 51 min.
35–54	27 h. 52 min.
55+	38 h. 22 min.
Children (both sexes)	
2–5	27 h. 49 min.
6–11	23 h. 39 min.

Nature of advertising for children's Saturday television programs, 1971 **

Type of product	Percent of commercials
Toys	23
Cereals	23
Candies or sweets	21
Other foods	23
Vitamins or medicine	1
Other products	9

Distribution of program elements in Saturday children's programs, 1971**

Program elements	Percent of time
Program content	77.3
Commercial announcements	
Commercial products	15.5
Program promotion	3.3
Noncommercial announcements	3.5
Other miscellaneous material	0.4

Viewing-time totals and achievement-test scores, 1982***

Hours (h) of TV per weekday	Reading scores	Writing scores
0	73	71
$0 \le h < \frac{1}{2}$	75	74
$\frac{1}{2} \le h < 1$	74	72
$1 \le h < 2$	73	72
$2 \le h < 3$	73	70
$3 \le h < 4$	72	70
$4 \le h < 5$	71	68
$5 \le h < 6$	70	68
$h \ge 6$	66	64

It is recommended that television be viewed from a distance greater than one meter (approximately 40 in.).

Viewing time per television-owning household

Year	Average time per day
1950	4 h. 35 min.
1951	4 h. 43 min.
1952	4 h. 49 min.
1953	4 h. 40 min.
1954	4 h. 46 min.
1955	4 h. 51 min.
1956	5 h. 01 min.
1957	5 h. 09 min.
1958	5 h. 05 min.
1959	5 h. 02 min.
1960	5 h. 06 min.
1961	5 h. 07 min.
1962	5 h. 06 min.
1963	5 h. 11 min.
1964	5 h. 25 min.
1965	5 h. 29 min.
1966	5 h. 32 min.
1967	5 h. 42 min.
1968	5 h. 46 min.
1969	5 h. 50 min.
1970	5 h. 56 min.
1971	6 h. 02 min.
1972	6 h. 12 min.
1973	6 h. 15 min.
1974	6 h. 14 min.
1975	6 h. 07 min.
1976	6 h. 18 min.
1977	6 h. 10 min.
1978	6 h. 17 min.
1979	6 h. 28 min.
1980	6 h. 36 min.
1981	6 h. 45 min.
1981–82	6 h. 48 min.
1982–83	6 h. 55 min.
1983–84	7 h. 08 min.
1984–85	7 h. 07 min.
1985–86	7 h. 10 min.
1986–87	7 h. 05 min.
1987–88	6 h. 59 min.
1988–89	7 h. 02 min.

* Source: A. C. Nielsen Co. (1990)
** Source: F. Earle Barcus, *Children's Television* (1977)
*** Source: *San Francisco Chronicle*, 21 July 1982

From the *Arithmetic Teacher*, May 1991

About the

Fingerprint Data Sheet

Directions

This data sheet should be duplicated and used with the class-activity sheet and the take-home family-activity sheet. The following information will help you and your students interpret the fingerprint data:

1. The classification of fingerprint-pattern types currently used by the Federal Bureau of Investigation (FBI) is based on the Henry system. This system recognizes three major categories of arches, loops, and whorls named according to the patterns made by the ridges of the fingers.

• *Arches.* The ridges in a *plain arch* (A) enter from one side of the finger, flow smoothly to form a curve resembling a hill in the center, and then exit the opposite side of the finger. The ridge pattern in a *tented arch* (T) is similar to a plain arch but forms a sharp upthrust that resembles a tent.

• *Loops.* Two pattern types are classified as loops: the *ulnar loop* (U) and the *radial loop* (R). In these two loop patterns, ridges enter from one side of the finger, curve to form a loop, and exit from the same side. These two loop patterns can cause some confusion because they are identified according to the hand from which the fingerprint is taken—left or right. With hands outstretched and palms down, as in taking fingerprints, one can identify two wrist bones in each arm. The ulna bone is at the outside edge of each wrist, nearest the little finger. The radius bone is at the inside edge of each wrist (see fig. 1). The loop fingerprints on each hand are identified according to whether they slope toward the ulna or the radius of that hand.

• *Whorls.* Four types of patterns are labeled as whorls. The ridges in the center of the *plain whorl* form a sort of whirlpool. Although the next two patterns have the word *loop* in their names, they are classified as whorls because the ridge lines do not enter

and exit on the same side of the finger. The *central-pocket loop* resembles a combination of an ulnar or radial loop and a plain whorl. The center of the *double-loop* pattern appears to form the letter S. Finally, the *accidental* pattern may bear some resemblance to the other patterns but not great enough to be classified as any of the others. Its ridges tend to enter from one side and exit on the opposite side.

2. Seven basic ridge characteristics are used to identify or match fingerprints. It is unlikely that any one fingerprint has all seven characteristics; however, it is very likely that a fingerprint has multiples of one characteristic. The *ending ridge* is a ridge line that ends suddenly. A *bifurcation*, or two-pronged fork, divides into two continuing ridges. Similarly, a *trifurcation*, or three-pronged fork, divides into three continuing ridges. A *dot*, or *island*, is a small ridge section that stands by itself. An *enclosure* briefly divides into two then returns to being one ridge, resembling the eye of a needle. A *bridge* is a short ridge that connects two ridges running roughly parallel to each other. A *hook*, or *spur*, divides into two, as in a bifurcation or fork, but one of the ridges is very short and ends suddenly. These seven characteristics are used in court as evidence of matching fingerprints.

3. Loops are the most frequently occurring patterns of fingerprints, followed by whorls and finally by arches.

Suggestions for taking fingerprints

The family activity and the extension to

the "Fingerprint Detective" activity require that students take their thumbprint. Here are some suggestions that will aid in taking prints:

1. Police departments and sheriff's offices typically are happy to send an "Officer Friendly" to classrooms to talk about his or her job. During such a visit, the officer could take fingerprints of students that would be kept by the students.

2. One method of taking fingerprints in the classroom uses a stamp pad inked with a dark color. Carefully press one finger at a time on the ink pad and then slide it over the surface of the pad. Press the finger onto white paper. Note that the "sliding" of the finger over the pad gives a much clearer print than just pressing the fingers on the pad. The latter approach tends to clump the ink.

3. Another method of taking fingerprints is to use black watercolor and a small paintbrush. Using the brush, carefully paint the surface of each finger and then press it onto white paper.

4. Teachers may find the following suggestions helpful in assisting students in taking their fingerprints:

• Practice taking your own prints first so that you can get a feel for what technique will work best with your own supplies.

• A clearer print can often be obtained by making more than one print from the same finger without reinking or repainting. If the ink is too heavy to get a clear print the first time, a second print can be made, resulting in a clearer image.

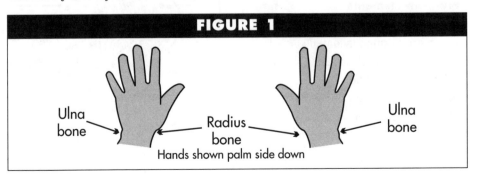

FIGURE 1

Ulna bone ← → Radius bone ← → Ulna bone

Hands shown palm side down

Fingerprint Data Sheet

Types of Fingerprint Patterns

Arches

Plain arch (A)

Tented arch (T)

Loops

Right-hand ulnar loop (U)
or
Left-hand radial loop (R)

Right-hand radial loop (R)
or
Left-hand ulnar loop (U)

Whorls (W)

Plain whorl

Central-pocket loop

Double loop

Accidental

Source: Federal Bureau of Investigation, 1990

Characteristics of Fingerprints

Ending ridge

Bifurcation
(Two-pronged fork)

Trifurcation
(Three-pronged fork)

Dot or island

Enclosure

Bridge

Hook or spur

Frequency of Occurrence of Patterns

Arches	5%
Loops	65%
Whorls	30%

Source: Federal Bureau of Investigation, 1990

From the *Arithmetic Teacher*, March 1991

Family Activities

Let's Work Together

FAMILY ACTIVITY

Objective

Students and parents work together to find solutions to mathematical puzzles

Materials

- A copy of the activity sheet "Let's Work Together"
- Scissors
- Optional: a large piece of construction paper, glue

Directions

1. Duplicate the activity sheet on construction paper.

2. Distribute a copy to each student to complete at home with a family member. If a family member is not available, students can choose another adult to whom they feel close.

3. Tell students to explain to their parents that the tangram puzzle on the activity sheet is a geometric puzzle that originated in China more than 4000 years ago. The object is to cut out the pieces and use them to form various figures.

4. Parents are asked to follow the directions on the activity sheet.

5. To build positive home-school communication, parents are asked to write a letter, with their child, to express their reaction to the mathematical experience.

6. Students could receive extra copies of the tangram puzzle from which to cut out and glue solutions on a large piece of art paper.

Extensions

1. The parent and child could describe their experiences with the mathematical investigations during a telephone conversation with another family member.

2. Follow the directions on the activity sheet to build such other shapes as a square, parallelogram, and pentagon.

Let's Work Together

Dear Family Members,

We have discovered many interesting things about geometry, especially the unique characteristics of triangles. During our study of geometry, we made triangles by solving problems or measuring and taping paper strips together. Some students have discovered interesting number patterns through their investigations. Communication skill in mathematics was enhanced by speaking, writing articles, and preparing make-believe television interviews.

Below is a set of geometric shapes. Let your child show you how many different geometric figures can be made with two, three, or four of the shapes. Work together to build triangles with two, three, four, five, six, and then all seven of the shapes. Make discoveries together. I would enjoy receiving a letter describing this mathematical experiment.

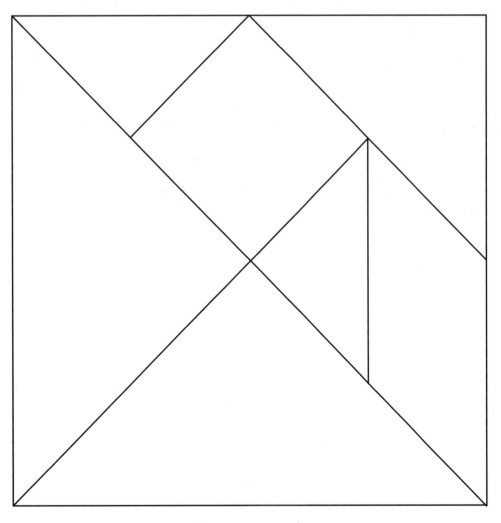

Tangram puzzle

From the *Arithmetic Teacher*, November 1993

IDEAS

Plastic Packaging

FAMILY ACTIVITY

Objectives

To gather and graph data, to interpret the graph, to develop a recycling plan

Directions

1. Show an item or two marked with a plastic recycling symbol. Use a disposable cup made of clear plastic or plastic foam, a plastic bag, or a plastic food package. Let the students find the symbol and note its number. Although plastic recycling numbers are voluntary, discuss why many manufacturers include them on new products. The recycling numbers occur in many places on plastic items and in no standard location.

2. Distribute a copy of the "Plastic Packaging" activity sheet to each student. Preview the directions. Suggest such qualities as color, thickness, and transparency for the students and their family members to notice in item 2 on the sheet. Ask the students to complete the activity sheets and bring them back to the classroom.

3. Ask the students to work in small groups to share their findings. Students can compile the total number of unmarked plastic items and the number with each marking. Have group representatives help to compile a chart or graph of the class's findings. Help students analyze the data, using the following questions:

- What is the range of numbers of plastic items in the categories?

- What decimal fraction or percent of the items was marked 2? 5? 7? Unmarked?

- If we repeated this activity using ten different containers from each family, do you think the results would be about the same or different? Why?

- If you walked into a store and picked up an item made of plastic, do you think it would or would not have a recycling number? Why? If it had a number, can you guess what the number would be? Why?

4. Invite the students to share some of their family's suggestions about conserving and recycling plastics.

Extensions

1. Students might copy and sketch the class results and report them to their family.

2. Students might repeat the activity at home, using more and different plastic products. They could then compare their predictions and graphs with the initial ones.

3. Students in grades 5–8 can interpret their family's and class's data using decimals and percents.

4. Students could use their family's data and make either a picture or a circle graph, for example.

112

Plastic Packaging

Dear Family Members,

In school, your child has participated in activities in which facts were gathered about common products we use and ordinarily throw away. This activity will let you, as a family, look at plastic products and decide on some ways to prevent wasting plastics.

1. Gather ten plastic containers or pieces of packaging material. Before you examine them, predict how many of them will have symbols like the one shown to indicate that it can be recycled. Record your prediction. _____

2. Examine the plastic items. What did you notice about the ones that have recycling markings? You may have found a number on the item from 1 to 7. Items marked with 1's are the easiest plastics to recycle; those marked with 7's are the hardest to recycle. _____

_____

3. Talk and write about what you notice as you examine the plastic items marked with recycling numbers. If you find more than one item with the same number, are their similarities and differences obvious? Can you tell by looking which items have higher or lower numbers? Write some ideas. _____

_____

4. Fill in the graph below to make a bar graph showing the number of containers of each type.

Markings on Plastic Containers

Markings		0	1	2	3	4	5	6	7	8	9	10
	No marking											
	♲1											
	♲2											
	♲3											
	♲4											
	♲5											
	♲6											
	♲7											

Number of Containers

5. Talk about your graph. Write down some things it shows. _____

_____

6. On the basis of your graph results, can you predict whether the next plastic item you pick up will have a recycling number? If it has a number, what will the number be? _____

7. Plastics are common materials. Often we throw them away without thinking. If we conserved and recycled, much energy and money could be saved. Discuss your uses of plastics and the ways in which you dispose of the items. Could you reduce your use? Could items and products that are easily recyclable be substituted for those items that are harder to recycle? As a family, make and implement a plan to conserve plastic.

From the *Arithmetic Teacher*, September 1993

IDEAS

A Consuming Activity

FAMILY ACTIVITY

Objective

To use a realistic situation as a means of collecting data

Directions

1. Reproduce a copy of the activity page for each student.

2. Have the students share the information with their family.

3. Encourage parents or guardians to help their children select food items for comparison.

Answers

Answers will vary. Students should be able to identify items such as fish or meat, which are purchased by the pound and often cost the same price, regardless of the quantity purchased. They may also find that some items have a higher unit price when larger quantities are purchased. This finding presents an opportunity to discuss the fact that larger containers do not always imply lower cost.

Extensions

1. As a follow-up activity to this exploration, bring in several food items from the grocery store and have students work in small groups to determine which items are best purchased in larger quantities. Observing small groups completing this task will give the teacher an opportunity to assess students' understanding of the concept.

2. Have students write an essay explaining why it is not good to purchase some items in larger quantities. What are some problems that occur when larger quantities of items are purchased? Which items require careful scrutiny when purchased in larger quantities?

Name _____

A Consuming Activity

Dear Family Members,

Unit pricing is an important concept for a consumer to understand. We have been discussing the fact that larger containers of food usually cost more but are actually more economical because the price per ounce or per pound is lower. To complete this activity, please take your child to a grocery store to record the data for the following questions. Then, working with your child and using a calculator, follow the instructions to complete the page.

1. Locate a candy or food item in the store that can be purchased in different quantities, such as a single-serving bag of SKITTLES or an individual box of raisins and large, family-sized bags or boxes. Record the price and weight of the item below:

The item we looked at was _____.

	Cost	Weight	Cost/Unit
Quantity 1	_____	_____	_____
Quantity 2	_____	_____	_____

2. Find any other two items in the store that can be purchased in two different sizes. You may want to compare, for example, a single shaker of salt with a box, or you may want to compare a small can of soup with a larger can. Record the items, their costs, and their weights below:

The first item we looked at was _____.

	Cost	Weight	Cost/Unit
Quantity 1	_____	_____	_____
Quantity 2	_____	_____	_____

The second item we looked at was _____.

	Cost	Weight	Cost/Unit
Quantity 1	_____	_____	_____
Quantity 2	_____	_____	_____

3. With your calculator, find the cost per unit for each of the three items that you have selected. To calculate, take the cost of the item and divide it by the weight (usually in ounces or grams), and round your answer to the nearest tenth of a penny. For example, an 8-ounce can that costs 67 cents would have a unit cost of 67 cents/8 ounces ≈ 8.4 cents per ounce.

4. Did you find that all three items were less expensive per unit when purchased in larger quantities? _____

5. Can you find an item in the store that is either the same cost or even more expensive per unit when purchased in a larger quantity? _____

Why do you think that this item is not less expensive per unit when purchased in a larger quantity? _____

_____

From the *Arithmetic Teacher*, April 1993

IDEAS

Station to Station

FAMILY ACTIVITY

Objective

To gain experience with likely or unlikely events, expected outcomes, or probabilities of events by collecting data on random events and making predictions

Directions

1. Discuss the music that students hear on the radio by asking such questions as the following: What types of music do you hear when you turn on the radio? If you chose a station at random, what type of music would you expect to hear?

2. List on the chalkboard all the types of music that the students think are played on radio stations. Some possible types of music are country and western, soul, blues, rock, rap, classical, jazz, and folk. You might decide to limit the number of categories to four or another reasonable number.

3. Distribute to each student a copy of the "Station to Station" activity sheet. Ask approximately half the students to circle "Please listen to AM stations" and the other half to circle "Please listen to FM stations." Have the students fill in the column heading on the chart with the types of music listed on the chalkboard.

4. Have students take home the "Station to Station" activity sheet. Ask students to record the results of this activity on the chart and bring it back so that their results can be combined and discussed in class.

5. Combine the results or have students do so. The students can devise an approach to find the class's totals in each category.

6. Explore analysis of data, probability, statistics, the notions of mode, and sampling by asking the following questions:

- If you chose ten stations at random, how many stations would you expect to be playing country and western music? Rock music?

- Do you think that if you repeated this experiment, you would get the same results? Do you think that the class totals would be about the same? Do you think that you would be able to predict which types of music are played most often? Least often?

- On the basis of the class's results, what is the probability of randomly choosing a station that would be playing rock music? Classical music?

Answers

Actual answers will vary and depend on the class's results.

Extensions

Students in grades 5 and 6 might use ratios or percent to determine the number of stations expected to be playing a particular type of music. Students in grades 7 and 8 should divide the number of occurrences of a particular type of music by the total number of musical selections counted to determine each probability. Students might express these probabilities as percents.

Name _____

Station to Station

Dear Family Members,

Your child's class has been studying some mathematical topics while learning about music. In the following activity, you and your child can investigate the various types of music that can be heard on the radio. You con do this activity at home or in your car.

      Please listen to AM stations.   Please listen to FM stations.

In an effort to increase information-analysis skills involving problem solving and reasoning, we shall discuss the results of this survey in class next week. Students in the class will combine their results and compare how frequently the various types of music were heard. They will also make predictions about what types of music are played most often in your geographic region.

1. The chart below lists several different types of music. Listen to the radio and decide which type of music you are hearing.

2. Tune your radio to some unfamiliar station that is playing music. After you have decided as a family which type of music you are hearing, make a tally mark in the column with that heading.

3. Listen to nine more songs by changing your radio to the next nine stations that are playing music.

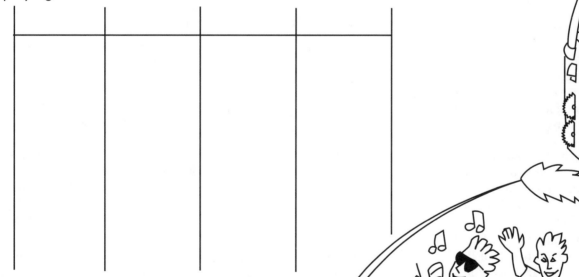

4. Look at the results. Are you surprised by what you found?

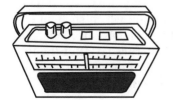

From the *Arithmetic Teacher*, December 1992

Exploring Election Calendar Dates

FAMILY ACTIVITY

Background

Although special and local elections are often held at several different times each year, presidential elections are always held at the same time—every four years on the first Tuesday after the first Monday of November. At the lower grade levels, students typically study the days of the week and calendar skills, whereas in the upper grades the actual date of a presidential election becomes more significant. This home activity lists a series of questions and explorations for a student to do with his or her parents or guardian that relate to the years and dates on which presidential and other elections fall.

Objectives

To enhance calendar skills, develop patterns, and explore divisibility and number theory

Directions

1. Explain to the class that presidential elections are always held in November and take place every four years. Also explain that by completing the activity page with their parents or guardian, students will learn more about the specific days on which elections are held and will discover some patterns. The students should take the activity sheet home and complete it with their parents or another adult.

2. When students bring the completed home-activity sheet back to school, discuss the solutions to the questions. Exploring the question about the 1996 election date will give teachers an opportunity to discuss leap year and the fact that an astronomical year is actually 365.25 days long. The last two questions concerning earliest and latest election dates and projecting their ages into the future may be too advanced for the younger students to understand. Discuss those questions with the class

that are practical and that relate to the local course of study.

Answers

1. The next three elections will be held in 1996, 2000, and 2004.

2. The November election dates are 3 November 1992, 2 November 1993, 8 November 1994, 7 November 1995, 5 November 1996, and 4 November 1997.

3. (*a*) Sunday, (*b*) Monday, (*c*) Tuesday, (*d*) Wednesday, (*e*) The day of the week advances one day each year. (*f*) 1 November 1996 falls on a Friday, which is a two-day advance. The reason is that 1996 is a leap year, which contains one extra day (29 February) that moves 1 November forward one day on the calendar.

4.

Nov. 1998

Su	M	Tu	W	Th	F	Sa
1	2	3	4	5	6	7
8	9	10	11	12	13	14
15	16	17	18	19	20	21
22	23	24	25	26	27	28
29	30					

Nov. 1999

Su	M	Tu	W	Th	F	Sa
	1	2	3	4	5	6
7	8	9	10	11	12	13
14	15	16	17	18	19	20
21	22	23	24	25	26	27
28	29	30				

Nov. 2000

Su	M	Tu	W	Th	F	Sa
			1	2	3	4
5	6	7	8	9	10	11
12	13	14	15	16	17	18
19	20	21	22	23	24	25
26	27	28	29	30		

5. The earliest possible first Monday of November would be on 1 November; therefore, the earliest election Tuesday would be 2 November. The latest possible first Monday of November would be 7 November, so the latest possible election day would be Tuesday, 8 November.

6. Answers will vary, depending on the ages of the parents and guardians and of the students.

Extensions

1. Discuss with the students the difference between local and national election issues. Ask the class to give examples of issues other than presidential elections on which voters cast a ballot (e.g., school levies, local mayoral races, gambling or lottery laws, library levies, etc.).

2. Have your students contact the local government offices to find out the possible dates on which nonpresidential elections can be held. For example, if the local school system needed to pass an emergency levy, what would be the possible dates on which such an election could be held? Is a formula, such as the first-Tuesday-after-the-first-Monday rule for presidential elections, used to choose these dates?

Name _____

Exploring Election Calendar Dates

Take this activity page home and complete the questions with your parents or guardian. Bring the page back to school for a discussion with the rest of the class.

1. A national election is held every four years to elect the president of the United States of America. If 1992 was an election year, in which years would the next three presidential elections take place? 1._____ 2._____ 3._____

2. The election for president of the United States is held every four years on the first Tuesday after the first Monday in November. To find this day begin by looking at the first Monday of November. The next day is the first Tuesday after the first Monday; therefore, it is the election day. Many areas hold an election on this day even in years when a president is not elected. Circle the November election dates on the calendars from 1992 to 1997.

Nov. 1992

Su	M	Tu	W	Th	F	Sa
1	2	3	4	5	6	7
8	9	10	11	12	13	14
15	16	17	18	19	20	21
22	23	24	25	26	27	28
29	30					

Nov. 1993

Su	M	Tu	W	Th	F	Sa
	1	2	3	4	5	6
7	8	9	10	11	12	13
14	15	16	17	18	19	20
21	22	23	24	25	26	27
28	29	30				

Nov. 1994

Su	M	Tu	W	Th	F	Sa
		1	2	3	4	5
6	7	8	9	10	11	12
13	14	15	16	17	18	19
20	21	22	23	24	25	26
27	28	29	30			

Nov. 1995

Su	M	Tu	W	Th	F	Sa
			1	2	3	4
5	6	7	8	9	10	11
12	13	14	15	16	17	18
19	20	21	22	23	24	25
26	27	28	29	30		

Nov. 1996

Su	M	Tu	W	Th	F	Sa
					1	2
3	4	5	6	7	8	9
10	11	12	13	14	15	16
17	18	19	20	21	22	23
24	25	26	27	28	29	30

Nov. 1997

Su	M	Tu	W	Th	F	Sa
						1
2	3	4	5	6	7	8
9	10	11	12	13	14	15
16	17	18	19	20	21	22
23	24	25	26	27	28	29
30						

3. Use the calendars to find out the day of the week on which 1 November falls. The first example is done for you.

(a) 1 November 1992 falls on *Sunday*. (b) 1 November 1993 falls on _____.

(c) 1 November 1994 falls on _____. (d) 1 November 1995 falls on _____.

(e) Explain the pattern that you have created for days of the week on which 1 November falls each year.

_____

(f) On which day of the week does 1 November 1996 fall? _____ Does this day fit your pattern? _____ Why or why not?_____

4. Create a calendar for the month of November for the years 1998, 1999, and 2000.

Nov. 1998

Su	M	Tu	W	Th	F	Sa

Nov. 1999

Su	M	Tu	W	Th	F	Sa

Nov. 2000

Su	M	Tu	W	Th	F	Sa

5. What is the earliest possible date in November on which a presidential election could be held? _____ The latest possible date? _____ Explain how you got your answers. _____

_____

6. In which year was your parent or guardian first able to vote for president (keep in mind that an individual must be 18 years of age to vote now)? _____ In what year will you first be able to vote for president?_____

From the *Arithmetic Teacher*, November 1992

Exploring Speed

FAMILY ACTIVITY

Background

Exploration is often a time-consuming endeavor. Historically, exploration has been conducted by boat, horse, and on foot, as well as through the use of modern rockets, satellites, and space shuttles. The purpose of this home-school activity is to give students an opportunity to investigate various modes of transportation and their effect on the amount of time required to conduct explorations. The students collect, record, and interpret data based on real-life information.

Objective

To develop skills in gathering and recording data, using tables, drawing and interpreting graphs, and at the upper grade levels, calculating the speed of travel

Directions

1. Distribute a copy of the "Exploring Speed" activity sheet to each student.

2. Discuss the many different modes of transportation used in exploration through the years. Whereas early explorers ventured on foot, such later explorers as Columbus traveled by ocean-going ship, and exploration of much of the American West was conducted on horseback or by river boats. Today, space shuttles and satellites are used for far-reaching exploration.

3. Interpret the table at the top of the "Exploring Speed" activity sheet. Discussion questions will vary, depending on grade level. For example, in the lower grades, students could be asked, "Did the Viking I travel to Mars before you were born?" or "Which trip took the longest time?" In the upper grades, students may be asked to calculate the speed of each exploration in miles per

day or miles per hour. The teacher should note that some distances on the chart are measured in nautical miles, whereas others are in statute miles. This issue need not be raised with students at this point unless the individual teacher wishes to do so.

4. Students should be encouraged to take the activity sheet home and complete the middle portion with the help of their parents. They should select one destination within two miles of their home and travel to it three times, using a different mode of transportation—driving, walking, biking, running, and so on—for each trip. Students should record the distance—perhaps as measured by the odometer on their parents' car—and the amount of time required for the trip. All the information is to be recorded on the table on the activity sheet.

5. When the students return the information to school, ask them to graph the information on the bar graph at the bottom of the activity sheet and answer the questions. Teachers may wish to encourage the parents to help the children construct the simple bar graph showing the time required to make the trip by three different modes.

6. Lead the class in a discussion of the information gathered. For example, in the lower grades, the questions might include these: "Which type of transportation was the fastest? The slowest?" In the middle grades, appropriate questions include "Did walking take more than twice as long as riding in the car?" In the upper grades, students could be asked to calculate the speed of each trip in miles per hour, dividing the distance by the fraction of an hour required to take the trip.

Answers

Answers will vary depending on the destinations chosen and the questions asked.

Extensions

1. Discuss with the class that although walking is often the slowest mode of transportation, at times it is the only practical mode available to an explorer. For example, if a vehicle is not available or if the terrain requires travel by foot, it may be necessary to walk.

2. In the lower grades. discuss other ways that travel might be timed. For example, a short trip can be timed by relating the distance to the number of times a favorite song can be sung before reaching the destination. A longer trip can be timed by imagining the number of episodes of a favorite television show one could view during the duration of the trip. Teachers might suggest these timing options for parents to use as they complete the activity page with their children.

3. In the middle or upper grades, have students use a calculator to compute the speed in miles per hour for each of the explorers in the chart at the top of the activity sheet. Students can compare the speeds of the various explorers and compare their own speeds for the various modes of transportation with those of the explorers. How do the explorers' speeds compare with the speed of walking or riding in the car?

4. In the upper grades, students can practice using exponents by calculating the speed of the Voyager I trip, working the exercise in scientific notation.

IDEAS

Name _____

Exploring Speed

The chart below includes data about some explorers from 1492 to 1979. Notice that two of the "explorers" are robots!

Explorers	Dates	Destination	Vehicle	Distance	Time	Speed
Columbus	1492	New World	Ship	4 300 mi.	37 days	
Lewis and Clark	1804–5	Pacific Coast	Canoe & Horseback	2 000 mi.	18 months	
Armstrong, Aldrin, and Collins	1969	Moon	Saturn V rocket	221 456 mi.	4 days	
	1975–76	Mars	Viking I	34 600 000 mi.	11 months	
	1977–79	Jupiter	Voyager I	390 700 000 mi.	18 months	

1. Who (what) do you think traveled the fastest? _____

2. Who (what) do you think traveled the slowest? _____

3. Identify a way to compare the travels of the various explorers._____

4. Use a calculator to help you figure out how fast each of the explorers traveled (speed can be found by dividing the distance by the time). Be careful to use the same unit of time for each explorer's trip if you plan to compare speeds.

You Be the Explorer!

Now it's your turn to collect some data. Ask your parents to help you choose a destination within two miles of your home. On each of three trips to your destination, use different modes of transportation. You might walk, ride a bike, skate, ride in a car, run, or use some other way that you can think of to get there. Have an adult help you measure the distance. Two ways you might measure the distance are using the odometer of a car and using the number of city blocks from your home to the destination. The adult can also help you keep track of the time required to get to the destination using each of the different modes of transportation.

Destination	Distance	Mode of Transportation	Time (Minutes)
1._____	_____	_____	_____
2. Same as above	Same as above	_____	_____
3. Same as above	Same as above	_____	_____

Using the information from your table, draw a bar graph below:

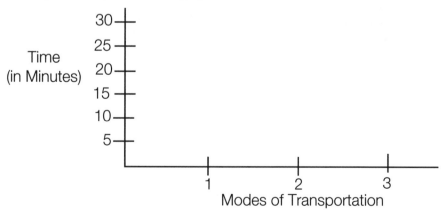

Which mode of transportation was the fastest for you? _____

Which mode of transportation was the slowest for you? _____

From the *Arithmetic Teacher*, October 1992

IDEAS

Shopping Spree

FAMILY ACTIVITY

Background

This series of activities begins with home involvement. Each student's family is asked to help find the prices for items on a list of school supplies. A number of appropriate activities are proposed to follow up after the activity has been completed and the results returned to school.

Objective

To collect, record, analyze, and orally and visually communicate data in various grade-appropriate ways

Directions

1. Duplicate the "Shopping Spree" family-activity sheet for each student in the class.

2. Explain to students that the family-activity sheet is to be taken home and completed with their parents or guardian. Make sure that students understand that the family-activity sheet will be used for various class activities after it has been returned to school.

3. Once the sheets are returned, compare the prices for each item, as indicated on the "Shopping Spree" fami-ly-activity sheet. Have students analyze the data in ways most appropriate for the experience levels of the class. For younger students, discuss the total number of items on the list. Use estimation to determine if twenty dollars would be enough to buy everything on the list. Discuss whether all students recorded the same price for a given item. Why might students have found different prices?

Using either today's prices, the early 1970s prices, or both sets of prices, have older students do the following:

(*a*) Find the total cost of all items.

(*b*) Calculate the range and median price, average price (mean), and typical price (mode) for a specific item.

Comparing the 1970 prices with today's prices, the students can do the following:

(*a*) Calculate the difference in prices between 1970 and today for specific items or for the entire list.

(*b*) Create a double-bar graph to illustrate the growth rate of prices.

(*c*) Find the percent of increase or decrease in price for each item from 1970 to today.

Have the students display the statistics they have gathered and discuss their information with classmates.

Answers

Answers will vary.

Extensions

1. Initiate a discussion of the prices of items that the students commonly purchase, such as candy bars, soft drinks, pizza, movie tickets, and video games. How have prices for these items changed over the years? Encourage the students to discuss price trends with their parents and be prepared to share the results with the class.

2. Invite the class to discuss the difference in a typical American's salary between the early 1970s and today. In 1971, the gross earnings of nonsupervisory workers in the United States was $121.00 per week and the minimum wage was $1.60 per hour. Older students can locate sources or authorities for corresponding figures for this year. Discuss the meaning of the term *comparable* and investigate whether today's prices are comparable to those of the early 1970s.

Name _____

Shopping Spree

Dear Family Members,

At school, your child is working on a back-to-school project. One of our objectives is to help your child become aware of the uses of mathematics in the world around us. As the new school year begins, a common mathematical experience for every student is the purchase of new school supplies. During this period, we will be talking in class about the costs of various school supplies and making comparisons with the costs of these materials in the early 1970s.

Please facilitate your child's finding the cost of each item on the list for her or his grade level in newspaper ads, in catalogs, or at a nearby store. Your child is to record the cost of each item and, using mental mathematics, paper and pencil, or a calculator, calculate the total cost of the items. With your child, please compare today's prices with the 1970 prices listed on the activity sheet.

It is important that your child return this activity sheet to school by next Monday because we will be using it in class to help us explore several interesting questions about the data. If you have any questions, please feel free to contact me at school.

Thank you.

Your child's teacher

Back-to-School-Item Record Sheet

Item	Today's Price	Early 1970s Price
1. Ten No. 2 pencils	_____	$ 0.03 each
2. Ruler with inch and centimeter markings	_____	0.10
3. One 64-count pack of crayons (gr. 3–6 only)	_____	0.99
4. Four-function calculator (K–6 only)	_____	89.95
Scientific calculator (7–8 only)	_____	149.95
5. One 4-ounce jar of glue	_____	0.22
6. Compass (4–8 only)	_____	0.29
7. Protractor (3–8 only)	_____	0.19
8. One 300-count pack of notebook paper (2–8 only)	_____	0.66
Six spiral notebooks (5–8 only)	_____	0.49 each
9. Two ball-point pens with blue ink (3–8 only)	_____	0.06 each
10. One each red, green, blue, and black felt-tipped pen	_____	0.25 each
11. One each red, blue, green, and black marker	_____	0.22 each
12. Five folders with pockets (3–8 only)	_____	0.19 each
13. One 100-count pack of 3 × 5 index cards.	_____	0.16

From the *Arithmetic Teacher*, September 1992

Computation Court: Home-Court Advantage

FAMILY ACTIVITY

This month's at-home activity sheet presents the situation of figuring the expenses for a vacation for a family of four, using alternative methods of transportation. Solutions and strategies for both alternatives are given. Students decide whether the solutions and the solution methods are correct and give reasons for their decisions. Encourage students to complete the activity sheet and to participate with their families in other real-world computations over the summer.

Answers

Case 1: Ramona's solution is incorrect.

Case 2: Raymond's solution is correct.

IDEAS

Computation Court:
Home-Court Advantage

Dear Family Members,

Your child has been studying computation, estimation, and mental mathematics in mathematics class. The summer months afford an excellent opportunity for the family to compute, estimate, and practice mental-mathematics skills while solving real problems. Two "computation court" cases are given to begin your summer computation. Ask your child, acting as the judge, to review each solution carefully and to pronounce a verdict—is the problem solved correctly? The verdict must then be justified by explaining how the decision was made. After these two cases have been resolved, you might involve your child in planning your summer activities. Have fun while giving your child the advantage of practicing computation and other mathematics skills over the summer.

Taking a Trip

Mr. and Mrs. Garcia have asked Ramona and Raymond to help them plan the summer vacation for the four of them to Philadelphia. Ramona is to determine the cost to go by car. Raymond is to figure the cost to fly. They will be gone for 14 days. The following information may be helpful:

1. The distance to Philadelphia is 1200 miles.
2. The Garcias' car gets 30 miles per gallon of gasoline.
3. Gasoline costs about $1.10 per gallon.

4. The airplane fare is $325 per person, round trip.
5. The average hotel room costs $75 each night.
6. Meals cost about $30 per person per day.

Ramona's solution

We will need about 400 gallons of gas, so that would be $400.40 for the gas. We will need to stay in a hotel for 13 nights, so that's about $1000 after adding the tax. Meals will be about $420. So the trip will cost a total of $1820.40. If we drive an average of 55 miles per hour, it will take us about 21 hours to get to Philadelphia and another 21 hours to get home, so we will need to spend about 5 days on the road.

Verdict: ☐ Ramona's solution is correct. ☐ Ramona's solution is incorrect.

Explain how you know. _____

_____

_____

_____

_____

Raymond's solution

For 4 people in the family, the airplane fare will be $1300. We won't need to eat out on the days we fly because we will get food on the airplane. Therefore, our meals will be $120 per day for 12 days, or $1440. The flight will take about 4 hours, so we will be in Philadelphia for 12 days and 13 nights. We will need to stay in a hotel for 13 nights, so that's about $1000 after adding in the tax. Therefore, the total cost will be $3740.

Verdict: ☐ Raymond's solution is correct. ☐ Raymond's solution is incorrect.

Explain how you know. _____

_____

_____

_____

_____

From the *Arithmetic Teacher*, May 1992

IDEAS

Gathering Graphs

FAMILY ACTIVITY

Background

The activities in this "Ideas" section include investigations of various graphs depicting real-world situations. This activity extends the investigation to discuss graphs and information from graphs that can be found in newspapers, magazines, or other printed material available in the home. The 1990 census data, which is used for the "History of Populations" activity, should be cut from the bottom of the sheet before the teacher sends it home.

Objectives

Students will work with their parents or another adult to—

1. find examples of graphs, and

2. discuss information in the graphs.

Directions

1. Reproduce a copy of the activity sheet for each student.

2. Have the students take home the activity sheet and complete it with their parents. Encourage the students to return the completed activity sheet to school to discuss any interesting observations that they made.

IDEAS

Gathering Graphs

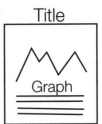

Dear Family Members,

Your child has been studying graphs in mathematics class. We have been looking at the information in graphs—the title, the words in the graph, and the numbers on the graph. We have been thinking about the steps used to make the graph and asking which graph best shows various types of information. We have emphasized trying to make predictions from graphs.

Parents can do the following graph-related activities with their child:

1. With your child, look through a newspaper, magazine, or book and select a graph.

2. Ask your child to read the title and tell what other words are written on the graph.

3. Have your child—

• cut out or copy the graph,

• paste it on a sheet of paper, and

• write some questions that con be answered by the graph.

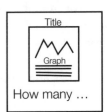

1990 Population Statistics by States

Rank	State	1990 Population	Rank	State	1990 Population
1	California	29 760 021	27	Connecticut	3 287 116
2	New York	17 990 455	28	Oklahoma	3 145 585
3	Texas	16 986 510	29	Oregon	2 842 321
4	Florida	12 937 926	30	Iowa	2 776 755
5	Pennsylvania	11 881 643	31	Mississippi	2 573 216
6	Illinois	11 430 602	32	Kansas	2 477 574
7	Ohio	10 847 115	33	Arkansas	2 350 725
8	Michigan	9 295 297	34	West Virginia	1 793 477
9	New Jersey	7 730 188	35	Utah	1 722 850
10	North Carolina	6 628 637	36	Nebraska	1 578 385
11	Georgia	6 478 216	37	New Mexico	1 515 069
12	Virginia	6 187 358	38	Maine	1 227 928
13	Massachusetts	6 016 425	39	Nevada	1 201 833
14	Indiana	5 544 159	40	New Hampshire	1 109 252
15	Missouri	5 117 073	41	Hawaii	1 108 229
16	Wisconsin	4 891 769	42	Idaho	1 006 749
17	Tennessee	4 877 185	43	Rhode Island	1 003 464
18	Washington	4 866 692	44	Montana	799 065
19	Maryland	4 781 468	45	South Dakota	696 004
20	Minnesota	4 375 099	46	Delaware	666 168
21	Louisiana	4 219 973	47	North Dakota	638 800
22	Alabama	4 040 587	48	District of Columbia	606 900
23	Kentucky	3 685 296	49	Vermont	562 758
24	Arizona	3 665 228	50	Alaska	550 043
25	South Carolina	3 486 703	51	Wyoming	453 588
26	Colorado	3 294 394		United States	248 709 873

Source: Census Bureau press release no. C891-100, 12 March 1991

From the *Arithmetic Teacher*, October 1991

Name_____

Television at Home

(Refer to "Television Data Sheet" on page 105.)

Dear Family Members,

Your child has been using mathematics in class while collecting and investigating data about television. Three additional activities are suggested on this sheet. You and your child may want to do one or more of them together. Check the accompanying data sheet to compare your data.

How Far from the TV Screen Do You Sit?

Do you sit a safe distance from the screen? Measure to find the distances from the TV screen that you and others in your home usually sit. Compare your measurements with the recommendation on the data sheet.

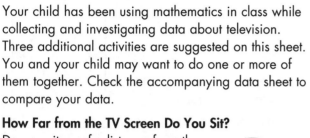

Keep a Family Viewing Log

For one week, keep a log of the times each person in your family watches television. Find the total viewing time for each person for that week. Compare the totals to those on the data sheet for the appropriate sexes and ages.

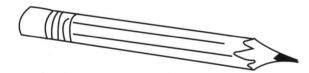

MONDAY EVENING	JOHN	SANDRA	MORGAN
5-6 p.m.	YES	No	YES
6-7 p.m.	NO	No	No
7-8 p.m.	YES	No	YES
8-9 p.m.	YES	YES	NO

What Do You Do during Commercials?

Survey your family, friends, and neighbors about what they do during commercials. Record your results in a chart.

Commercial Viewing and Listening

Action	Tally	Number of People
Watch and listen		
Watch only (Turn sound off)		
Listen only		
Neither watch nor listen (Leave room, etc.)		

From the *Arithmetic Teacher*, May 1991

Fingerprints at Home
(Refer to "Fingerprint Data Sheet" on page 107.)

Dear Family Members,

Your child has been using fingerprints to investigate such mathematical ideas as patterns in nature. This sheet shows several different activities that use fingerprints. You and your child could select one or more of the activities to do together.

You will need—

• a copy of the "Fingerprint Data Sheet,"
• a magnifying glass or a pair of reading glasses, and
• an ink pad or dark watercolors.

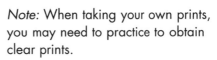

Three Methods for Obtaining Prints

Follow one of these methods to obtain prints:

1. Visit your local sheriff or police station and have your fingerprints taken. You will be given the copy.
2. Slide fingertips over an ink pad, then press onto white paper.
3. Use a small paintbrush to paint fingertips with dark watercolor paint, then press onto white paper.

Note: When taking your own prints, you may need to practice to obtain clear prints.

Take thumbprints of all family members, and label them with the name, left or right thumb, and the type of pattern (see the data sheet). In your family, whose thumbprints are of the same pattern as yours? Look at all the thumbprints you took. Which type of pattern occurs most often—arches, loops, or whorls?

Go to the library. Find books about fingerprints. Some science books and books about the body have such information.

Two of the thumbprints below are identical. Which are they? _____ and _____

Thumbprint A	Thumbprint B	Thumbprint C	Thumbprint D	Thumbprint E

From the *Arithmetic Teacher*, March 1991